WAR IN THE HEARTS OF MEN

ELI COBERLY

FROM THE TINY ACORN ...
GROWS THE MIGHTY OAK

www.AcornPublishingLLC.com
For information, address:
Acorn Publishing, LLC
3943 Irvine Blvd. Ste. 218
Irvine, CA 92602

War in the Hearts of Men
Copyright © 2022 Eli Coberly

Edited by Laura Taylor
Cover design by Damonza
Interior design and formatting by Debra Cranfield Kennedy

Printed in the United States of America

ISBN-13: 979-8-88528-021-1 (hardcover)
ISBN-13: 979-8-88528-020-4 (paperback)

PREFACE

A fter failing in relationships more often than I've succeeded, I realize that on this planet our current model of masculinity is not working. I felt the experience of this truth so deeply, it became impossible to ignore. Through my own trauma from military service and my personal search for truth, I found a way to internally transform myself, not just through the physical practice of yoga, but in keeping with the philosophy of the religion of yoga, which isn't limited to the Far East.

The questions I asked at the beginning were, "If the snake was such a big part of evolution and revered by cultures worldwide, then why in the Bible is it associated with Satan and evil? And why is it associated with the projection of guilt for women?"

I felt the need to be more than just the change I wished to see in the world. I felt the urge to serve as a beacon to correct the imbalance of the sexes and the manifestations of war.

ACKNOWLEDGMENTS

Behind the scenes were brothers in editing, Matt, Derrick, and Richard. Of all the rat's nests to navigate—thanks, y'all, for navigating this one. To Marla . . . thanks for the structure.

1

WHAT A LONG, STRANGE TRIP IT'S BEEN

It was in the fall of 1996 when I arrived at my first Army duty station at Fort Bragg, North Carolina. I walked into the barracks to witness a man smoking a cigarette in the hallway. The smoke burnt his eyes as the glow in the dimly lighted hallway illuminated his face. The ash piled on the floor and it swirled down the tile as chiseled bodies clad in camouflage poured out of their rooms. I followed the path of smoke and ash, visually connecting last names with faces.

His hand shook from withdrawal. As he cleaned his M-60, a bead of alcohol-infused sweat dripped from his nose. It seemed to fall in slow motion into the chamber.

I watched in awe.

"Hey, Cherry, my name's Hess."

"Everyone, say hi to the new cherry," said the platoon sergeant.

Just then a man of my same rank asked me to do push-ups.

"No," I answered.

This didn't sit well with anyone.

Over the next week I was harassed more and more, especially when they found out I could do more pushups and run faster than they. I wanted their acceptance and, more than anything, their trust. But I was torn between acting tough and being a pushover.

As soon as it hit five o'clock, most of the other soldiers were downing Bud Lights and chain smoking. Usually around midnight a few of them started to yell Babalu. I was unsure what that meant. Each night it became louder and louder.

One night I heard pounding on my door.

"Hey, it's Ted. Let's party; we have beer," I heard through the door.

"Hell, yeah," I said.

I was thinking they'd accepted me. This would be a bonding experience. Standing in my underwear at the door, I unlocked the deadbolt. Ten guys wearing black leather gloves—some masked and some not—rushed me, pinned me down, and someone locked the door. I knew exactly who they were.

They shut out the light for a second, but it seemed like an eternity. It was silent. Then they began to chant.

"Bob aloo, bob aloo."

The chants grew louder and louder. My hands and feet were restrained, my eyes covered by a towel. I smelled rubbing alcohol in the darkness. As I peered from under my blindfold, I saw the black gloves illuminated and burning in blue flame. Their hands began to beat my upper torso with great force.

In tears I took the beating. I was powerless and silent. It was the worst pain I had ever felt. I gasped as one of them cupped a hand over my mouth. Something alerted the sergeant downstairs at the front desk. They must've heard him coming, because they all fled at once.

"Coberly, are you okay?" he yelled as he entered the room.

"I'm fine; I fell off the top bunk," I said, still in tears.

"Bullshit, go to bed. We'll deal with this in the morning," he said.

Just as soon as I closed my eyes, they were reopening. I heard a loud banging on the door.

Sergeant Bromly, the guy from the night before, yelled, "Get the fuck up, were going to the First Sergeant's."

"Just to let you know, Hess and Mcguff are already standing tall before the man," he whispered in my ear as we walked down the stairs.

I felt sick to my stomach, not only because of the pain from my beating, but because I knew they were aware of what had happened. I would be either hated for the rest of my enlistment, or I could keep my mouth shut. I had to make a choice in that instant.

Sergeant Bromly opened the door and the wind pulled me to the desk. I screeched to the position of attention and saluted the company commander.

"At ease, Coberly. What the fuck! Lift up your shirt," he ordered.

I looked to my left. Bromly, Hess and Mcguff were all at parade rest just like I was.

I took a deep breath. Before I exhaled, the First Sergeant chimed in, "You heard the man."

I pulled up my gray army shirt and the First Sergeant yelled, "Jesus fucking Christ, what the hell happened?"

I looked and saw handprint on top of handprint in every color of the rainbow.

"I fell off my bunk," I answered.

"Bullshit, try again," replied the First Sergeant.

I froze.

"I'm not going to ask you twice!"

I looked over at the other guys. In an instant, I pictured a long hellish time out in the field on training exercises.

The captain winced as I cleared my throat. "It's like I said, sir."

The First Sergeant, a crusty lifer, smirked behind his mustache, as if saying that he liked my style. Nevertheless, I was busted down two Ranks. I was court martialed for lying to an officer. But for me it was worth it, because I gained the trust of the rest of the group forever. And I buried that memory the best I could.

Many years later in the spring of 2021, I still felt pain from a broken rib where I had slipped and landed on a cosmic two-by-four. This time it was an actual two-by-four. The piece of lumber, sticking up from the ground vertically, went under my solar plexus. I was certain it had pierced my heart. Sprawled on the ground, I stared at the sky as I took a shallow breath.

"Mother!" In agony, I tried to yell.

I decided I wasn't going to die, and it was probably just a broken rib. My neighbor drove me to the emergency room, where they confirmed the fractured rib.

In August of that year, I headed back to Raleigh, NC to visit my Army friends as the United States finally withdrew from Afghanistan. I sat in my seat on the plane, feeling a jolt to my solar plexus and a pain in my rib.

I often meditate on flights to relax. When I meditated on this flight, I remembered both the experience of the beating of my solar plexus and the cosmic two-by-four reminders.

Winston Churchill once said, "Those who fail to learn from history are condemned to repeat it."

The cosmic two-by-four counseled me to remember the past and to speak my sovereign truth. In my personal life I had leased a property that was about to be repossessed, because the lessor did not own it. I was about to lose most of my retirement, for which I'd worked for more than half my life. My business partner asked me to give him everything so he could succeed, and I could lose.

He was like every other large man I had interacted with. He was in it for himself. He viewed me as inferior, because of my smaller size and because of my interest in love, friendship, and camaraderie above money.

Whether true or false, I learned unequivocally several times during my life that large white men can do what they want in business. Business is the modern-day version of violent slavery. And if I wanted to succeed in that world, walking away in peace was the best strategy instead of using violence as a means to an end.

The cultural irony has always been that I could simply destroy a man with my bare hands if he rips me off, or I could carve him up with a knife just like the government taught me to do. I learned that passive violence is just as bad, because it is justified by the lies of society. The emotional pain of this truth was manifested in my third Chakra of the ego as a lack of willpower. The opportunity for change was at the forefront of my mind.

The next day I sat in a Suburban with my fellow Airborne Infantry vets and the father of one, a former Green Beret trainer. Before we left for the *Dead and Company* show, he put his Glock with a high-capacity magazine and two ounces of psilocybin mushrooms in the fridge. I guess he wanted to keep things on ice. Guys with this kind of knowledge are never over it, always perceiving the next threat in an unconventional way.

Thunder and lightning shook the earth and illuminated the sky. The rain came down as we sat in the vehicle, waiting to get through traffic. All of us were in agreement about a premature withdrawal in Afghanistan. Not because we wished for more war, but because of the waste of our brothers' efforts and lives.

The mushrooms started to kick in for Bob Senior, and we talked about the political climate in the US being ripe for a coup d'état. He saw weakness and a lack of follow-through. The troops he'd trained had gone to Afghanistan to train the locals to fight the Taliban and win with unconventional warfare.

"They were on target in the beginning," he said.

"What happened?" I asked.

"Well, it's simple. The US, just like the Russians and Chinese, wanted the vast resources under Afghanistan. The Pentagon didn't seem to think that winning so quickly would be the best or quickest way to the cool one trillion. We thought we could get to it in less than ten years by being diplomatic about war. Boy, were we wrong!"

Figure 1. Symbol of the Pentagon,
Pentagon, Department, Defense Icon
(via shutterstock.com)

2

TIME AND TRAUMA

While waiting in line for the show, one of the other ex-paratroopers, Mitch, and I spoke about his medical retirement. I remembered that he once went out the door of a perfectly good C-130 airplane over a North Carolina drop zone. He blacked out, and when he came to, was the only one left.

He recounts the story.

"It was one of the largest drops we did over Ft. Bragg."

We boarded the plane, dripping in olive drab equipment. The plane ended up circling the drop zone, taking forever. It was now 1.5 hours later, and I started to feel the effects. It was supposed to be a 20-minute flight.

The jumpmaster checked the door for any obstructions, grabbed the edge of each side of the door and leaned out to check that the plane was over the drop zone. He yelled at us to hook up and, as usual, we echoed his command then fastened the hooks to the main cable running down each side of the door. The red light above the door turned green. Weighted down with equipment, I exited the aircraft. The g forces, as usual, sucked me out the door with the other jumpers.

In a few seconds my parachute opened . . . I checked for a full canopy and noticed that, not only was my chute not fully deployed, but I was also falling rapidly. I was weaving in and out of the suspension lines of others and trying to get control of my canopy.

Now, I feared for my life. At this moment I considered pulling my reserve. By the time I made the decision not to, I pulled a cord to lower my equipment. As soon as it hits the ground, so do I, first with my feet then my head.

The next thing I remembered was waking up on my back in the dark. We had jumped right before dusk. I released my chute and decided to link up with the rest of the company. I guess I was more afraid of what would happen to me for not showing up in the assembly area than how damaged my body was.

My entire upper right side was unusable. I put on my ruck-sack, grasped my M-4 carbine and moved out. Then I double-timed it back to the barracks to catch up with the rest of the paratroopers. By the time I reached the main thoroughfare, I spotted the tail end of the soldiers. I then saw First Sergeant Love running toward me and cussing.

"What the fuck?" he yelled. "Put down your goddamn weapon, remove all your gear and stand by."

I immediately passed out.

The next thing I saw were faint lights becoming brighter. I couldn't move. It seemed like I was in an institution of some sort. They put me in traction as I began to scream.

Seeing the face of a woman, I said, "I've been here for hours. Help! Help!"

"Sir," she responded. "It's only been three minutes since we did your intake."

"Get me the fuck off this thing," I yelled.

Minutes later, they confirm that I had a concussion and hand me a few bottles of narcotics. I get a ride back to the barracks the following day. Desperately hoping that the pain will subside, I take as many of the pills as I can stomach."

This is just one story I am presenting about the lack of interest in the soldier's well-being. The expendability of our teenage boys is real.

Military static line parachuting is a whole other ballgame compared to civilian freefall skydiving. With military static line jumping, the shoot deploys after five seconds and the soldier is typically on the ground within a few minutes. It's a very short time in which to react to numerous things that can and will go wrong.

I recalled another of those times while I made a stop in Washington, D.C., to see Embury, another Army comrade of mine. We spent the next twenty-four hours at a couple of bars and a Chinese restaurant. We both smoked hash, and he smoked a cigarette just as I remembered he used to. Inhaling deeply in between nostalgic thoughts of others, he swilled the booze and shared his memories. The following is one such account of memory for Mitch, Embury, and me.

We were tasked to participate in a multi-Brigade jump called Operation Purple Dragon. The enlisted men like me immediately coined it Purple Barney. The size and scope of this jump was like no other. As always, I was ready to get the fuck out of the "bird." My entire body would fall asleep from the weight of the equipment resting on my lap. The jump master yelled "Hook up!"

I was near the back of the plane. "Hook up!" I yelled back in unison with the rest of the jumpers as I connected my line to the cable. As I got halfway to the front, the green light switched back to red. And it was announced that we had a tow jumper.

A tow jumper is just as it sounds—the jumper is being towed by his static line while his body gets beaten up against the side of the fuselage of the plane. The standard operating procedure is, if the jumper is conscious, the jumpmaster cuts his static line which deploys the main parachute. That way he can pull his reserve and, with any luck, land relatively safely. I saw Embury—who had been with me at Basic Training, Airborne School and now at the same duty station—exit the door up ahead.

I exited soon after the chute deployed and checked my canopy. The sky was full of little green men hanging like puppets.

I usually took longer than most to land since I only weighed 135 lbs. This time I kept hitting pockets of air. I was descending fast. I ran across the top of two jumpers' canopies in a row and oscillated between another's suspension lines. Hitting the ground hard, I released my chute as it was a hop-and-pop.

In the darkness I began to move out. I heard a scream, and what sounded like a little boy sobbing. When I and a few others moved toward the light on the drop zone, I saw my friend shining the light on what looked to me like a turkey at Thanksgiving. In the dark was an illuminated corpse. It was the tow jumper. Embury, who had jumped ahead of me, was the one shining the light.

Frozen, I observed the outline of an upper torso with what I thought was a broken femur sticking out of it. Mitch also stood there with tears in his eyes, and he immediately tore his jump wings from his fatigues. I remember thinking, this is just a training exercise, not a war. This isn't supposed to happen. But in reality, it did. I joined Embury and assembled with our platoon leader at the rally point.

The soldiers closer to the body saw much more graphic details. This young paratrooper was split wide open from his hips to his neck. The skin from his face was peeled back and his femur was broken with a jagged end sticking up vertically. They all frantically tried to help this poor soul. They began to remove his jump harness and gear, almost as if to free him from the pain. But there's no pain when someone is dead.

Embury was set to go to NCO (non-commissioned officer) school the following week. The death shook us all to our cores. Embury continually prayed to God for our brother's family. The dead soldier wasn't an infantryman like us. He was a combat engineer. These guys typically placed explosives to blow a breach in the concertina wire. He was survived by his single mother. Embury later found out from our platoon leader that he was of the Christian faith.

"Listen, you have more of a chance of dying in a car accident than a jump! It's not going to fucking happen to you. You're going to make it, and you're going to school," Staff Sergeant Deleon told him.

Embury was put on day jumps with what we called pogues. They were noninfantry—weak, in our minds. We often yelled at them, calling them shitbags as they fell out of Division runs. Deleon thought that this would restore Embury's confidence. The fact is, all of us were afraid to die and, for me, every jump increased my terror. I felt that I was rolling the dice each time. Mitch and Embury received zero psychological counseling. Neither did any of us, including that pogue officer bawling like a baby.

As I said, we often trained with the combat engineers. On one such exercise a few months later, we were tasked to take out a bunker complex at Ft. Bragg. It was, once again, our battalion acting as a larger force in cooperation with many other units. The objective was to parachute then walk through the jungle towards the bunker complex.

The engineers were to employ a Bangalore torpedo and blow a breach in the six strands of concertina wire sky high, so we could enter the breach and assault the bunker complex. There was a whole platoon in between me and the breach. Up on the hill the M-60 machine gunners provided not only cover fire, but also hammering the many bunkers positioned a few hundred meters in front of me.

This was business as usual for all of us. The guns provided fire, and we flanked the enemy. Only this time a man was shot. The young private in front ran into a half-dozen 7.62mm bullets. I guess he went quick.

We walked back into the jungle where we were told that a man only eighteen was dead from friendly fire. They didn't court-martial anyone, Mitch explained twenty-two years later, because the investigation showed that the engineer had prematurely run through the breach, which was when Mitch saw him get lit up. He described the death as a poof of red and the guy just kind of exploded.

Mitch was part of Sergeant Jewett's squad. In this particular squad, half the personnel had Ranger tabs. This sort of elevated a soldier for more opportunities. It was as if the senior enlisted and officers were grooming the rest of the squad, and eventually the company, to follow suit. Sergeant Jewett was a small man with no neck, and he had what I considered a psychotic-sounding laugh. To me, Jewett was an out-of-control hillbilly.

Come to find out, in 2011, he told his wife to get the dogs out of their bed and she refused, so he cocked his .45 and fired a round into each dog, killing them instantly. Soon after, his wife fled south to Florida, and he tracked her down and murdered her. He is now serving life.

The military chooses from the poorest and least-educated. They are the ones from small towns and ghettos who don't have many options. This is especially true with the infantry, because you don't have to score high on the tests to get in. Many of them, like myself, were looking to get out of a bad or limiting situation.

These people are dealing with ancestral trauma that has and will manifest in their relationships. We see them parentless or abused, and this plays out in their world view. So the already trauma-impacted brain becomes loaded with samskaras, an ancient yogic concept. These are long-held impressions. The habit is for the individual to become closed emotionally when the senses perceive a threat.

Each emotional center will perceive a threat based on its last experience, and the individual will react in the same way as previously. The go-to response creates a lack of emotional growth in the related chakra, or wheel. In the center of the chakra, which is represented as a spiral, is the zero point where anything is possible. In this space and context, healing can occur because in the center is the inception of the incident. Rather than the mind creating more experiences based on the original traumatic event, it creates a new experience.

I will use Mitch as an example. He has subluxations in his spine. Some in his cervical as well as his lumbar. Years later, he found out that he had broken his neck from that jump where he blacked out. The emotional and physical pain was just too much to bear. Mitch, like me and countless others, had a difficult time coping after his separation from the Army.

He did the paperwork to get fully disabled, but he just couldn't trust his doctors and especially his psychiatrist. When I went to visit, he told me that he trusted me one hundred percent. We were brothers, and I was his confidant.

I will attempt to explain a very complex theory about energy and healing from my perspective.

Dreams are portals to deep subconscious wounding that's rooted in a trauma. I told Mitch about this, and he told me about his recurring dreams. The psychiatrist he had at the VA asked him to relive his trauma in every session. That he had to reset his relationship to it. While I believed this to be true and viable, I had another suggestion.

I asked him if he could remember any of his dreams. Come to

find out he had nightmares about being dragged away by hooded figures. They were gripping his feet and dragging him through a wall.

I told him that if time was cyclical and not linear, then he could go back to the original event in the dream and change it if he so desired. Also, that I wanted to use my dowsing rods on him.

We sat and talked about the past, the present, and the future. I told my comrade about the time in Guatemala where I studied the Akashic records with Ernesto Ortiz. Then I further explained the concept of Akasha in the context of the center of the spiral. The place of no time. We busted out the dowsing rods and went to work. I energetically tuned into his subtle energy body as I held the L-shaped copper rods. They began to spin.

As with any energetic practice, the individual must believe in the method. It seemed that he did. When I moved the rods from the top of his head to his tailbone, they began to point to the places where he had broken his neck and his lower back. I feel as if this tells me where the water could go. Where the path of easiest resistance could flow that has been blocked, much like the Chinese describe chi.

In essence I see a unique path for healing for those who are willing. We are mostly made up of water, and we are electrical beings taking up energy from the center of the earth's magnetic core. The more electricity, the more opportunity for healing. When a vertebra subluxation occurs, then the nerve channels or Nadis are usually blocked or impeded.

The interesting thing about spinal pain is that one person will be virtually paralyzed with it and another with the same condition will be pain-free. The difference is most likely the mind's relationship to the story of how the injury occurred. It sort of grips and grasps onto the emotional content and won't let go. So, what is actually occurring here, and how does it help corroborate a story of healing?

Mitch decided on a possible pain-free life by confronting his shadow, especially the shadow figures in his dream. He decided that it could be possible to change the outcome of his story to include a path of healing. This seed could be planted not only for his ancestors but for his children. And maybe with just a little water, the seed will grow roots.

My brief stop in D.C. had me reflecting on the shadow side of war. If war manifests in relationships, then it is safe to say that it is also expressed through religion and even architecture.

The Pentagon has a blatant representation of the five-pointed star and Pentateuch in reflection of Semitic culture. While across the city is the Washington Monument, a stone tribute to Egypt's obelisks. Even the White House stands in remembrance of Rome and ancient Greece with its large white columns.

Through war, we take on the energetics and vibration of cultures of the past and project them onto the shadow of the collective. It is almost as if we are saying, "We too will be a great civilization like the culture whose symbols we've recycled. We, too, will have our evil actions justified by God and religion. From these actions our offspring can thrive and carry on our legacy."

3

THE SERPENT

I t was 2006 in Belize. My wife and I were honeymooning in the Mayan ruins of Caracol.

The sun peeked out above the clouds, giving them golden edges. The jungle path beneath my feet turned to grass, and as I looked up, my eyes saw their first Mayan pyramid.

Sidetracked by a pepper plant on the edge of the jungle, I took a bite of one of the tiny red fruits.

"Hot, hot!" I jump up and down.

"Let's go up the pyramid." said my wife, Haley.

"What does Caracol mean?" I asked.

"Spiral or something," she replied.

"What does Maya mean?" I asked, breathless as we reached the top of the pyramid.

"It's Sanskrit for the illusion," she tells me.

A decade later, I was solo. It was 2016, and I had been studying yoga, meditation and mysticism for a number of years. I would spend a bit of time in Mexico doing such pursuits at the pyramids.

I noticed a special energy present there that seemed similar to what the ancients described as Kundalini, the energy of the serpent. I started to see snakes scribed in the stucco art of the pyramids and stelae.

Halfway from Tulum to Campeche, I hid from the sun in a taco stand on the side of the road, waiting for the *comida*. On the pavement I saw a chicken that looked virtually reptilian; he was pecking in the cracks.

Missing the pleasures and pains of tequila, I reflected. Throughout time and space in our evolution as a species, mysteries have served as the cornerstone of the human spiritual journey. They are a constant state of inquiry into the void. The roots of unknown territory, once excavated, can act as a map for a collective subconscious, which in turn results in a greater understanding of the individual as part of a whole.

Transformation through mythological symbolism can unlock our perception of who we think we are and propel us into who we are destined to become. I believe that most of humanity's struggles have taken place so that we might become closer to our essence.

What if we had a greater knowledge of the roots of humanity?

In the beginning, according to Genesis in the Bible, man was created in God's image and from him, woman. The foundation of our failing societies' entire philosophical truth rests on this teaching.

After Adam and Eve ate from the tree of knowledge, God gave them access to the Tree of Life, i.e. immortality. What is the origin of the tree? How many times have we felt really good, and yet, couldn't help but feel guilty for it?

When Eve was in the Garden of Eden, God forbade her

through Adam from eating from the tree of knowledge for fear of death. That same Tree of Life served as the tree of divinity for many other cultures. The Incans, the Vikings, the Hebrew, the Buddhists, and pretty much every other major civilization with religion has had a version of the Tree of Life. Eventually, the tree became the cross and humanity was nailed on it for our sins.

Nicola Tesla once said, "If you want to find the secrets of the universe, think in terms of energy, frequency and vibration."

Ancient traditions knew of this energy when the scientific method was less than a priority, thousands of years before the invention of the computer. Perhaps water is the key, and the serpent is the vehicle.

If you take a flight to Cancun, Mexico, chances are you're going to see lush jungle and white sand with crystal blue water. Sprawling up from the jungle, the city itself is a tourist trap with nonstop harassment to dine at restaurants, drink overpriced booze, and live the good life on your vacation.

One of the tours you might get talked into is that of Chichen Itza. Despite the unruly crowds, it is well worth a visit and one of the most popular Mesoamerican sites. This Post-Classic era archeological find contains remnants of the serpent dynasty. Within the very center of this ancient Mayan "university" is El Castillo. The Maya called it the Temple of Kukulkán, which means the "place where the serpent dwells."

As with most Mayan mythology, especially that which surrounds the Kaan Dynasty, it is hard to discern between a cosmic metaphor and the actual ruler or teacher in human form. There are many Maya living today in the Yucatan and beyond, who believe that Kukulkán was a man. The Spanish conquest and their attempt to eliminate the rich history of this ancient culture forced us to rely on archeology and oral history.

The Late-Classic city of Chichen Itza is an echo from the past. That echo resonates back to Teotihuacan, a city that embodied Quetzalcoatl, the feathered serpent deity. The pyramids are decorated with the heads and bodies of plumed serpents.

From what archeologists can tell, the Kaan Dynasty installed puppet rulers in strategic locations throughout what is now Quintana Roo and Campeche, Mexico, and Guatemala. Not much is known about this elusive outfit. They had ties to the city of Teotihuacan, and they were very influential in the land of the Maya. It is generally agreed that the seat of this great dynasty was in Calakmul, Mexico.

In Mayan art and architecture, hieroglyphs were used as markers for the names of rulers as well as groups. Much of the proof of the dynasty's expansion and control was found in 2016 at several sites in Guatemala, Mexico and Belize. Kaan is a Mayan word for serpent, and glyphs from the Kaan were found at what is now southern Mexico and northern Guatemala. As is the case with most archeological discoveries, tombs and records of the past were found under the temples at these sites.

Their local history is not only literally buried, but culturally submerged as well. If you ask the average person on the street in the surrounding cities about the Kaan Dynasty, they are familiar with the meaning of the word Kaan as serpent, but there is no common knowledge of the ancient rulers. When I began my search, I noticed something completely different than I ever anticipated.

4

THE SEARCH

I learned that the Maya's wars, like most, were initiated to establish control over the land's precious resources for trade and agriculture, which meant control of Mother Earth. Before the invasion of the serpent kings using a sacred symbol, the feminine played an altogether different role. Many recorded dates of feminine rulership are cemented in time on stelae, or stone monuments, spread throughout central America.

Hot on the trail of the serpent dynasty, I was headed to a puzzle piece of a mystery that lies south of Calakmul in present-day Guatemala. My research had me en route to a place called Sak-Nikté, which translates to "white flower." To date, this metropolis could have been the most passive of all in Mesoamerica. I was curious what they did differently and how their history paralleled modern colonialism.

Brides and grooms were exchanged between the peoples of Sak-Nikté and Calakmul. These unions were instrumental in creating faith in their shared dictatorship. Having strong ties insured a future free from the invasions of rival dynasties.

In 2016, after being refused entry at the Guatemala border in a Mexican rental car, I decided to follow another lead. Xpujil is the nearest town to Calakmul and located on the horn of the southern tip of Mexico, halfway between the Caribbean Sea and the Gulf. I was definitely off the beaten path—courtesy of a rising feral dog population, seemingly growing by the minute. The littered streets masked the strangely alluring scent of cheap laundry soap, tortillas, and barbecued chicken.

In the very center of town stood a twelve-foot-tall cement statue of a woman, suggesting a strong feminine resonance in the local population. Buried beyond this unique byproduct of Spanish conquest, deep in the jungle lies Calakmul: the doorway to the seat of the Kaan Dynasty. The following day I would open that door.

In the morning, the road to Calakmul was thick with fog and smelt of burning wood and plastic—most of the locals had started fires to burn their garbage. The site itself was nearly three hours from the town, and has a permanent nature reserve the size of Singapore.

The roads were full of turkeys, monkeys, tapirs, and other animals. The archeological site had over eight "sacbes"—"white roads"—leading from pyramid to pyramid, but one that also ran south to none other than El Mirador. The discovery in 1926 of the ruins of this cradle of the Mayan civilization revealed a record of the creation story that predated Christianity by at least one hundred years.

It was the dry season. I felt leaves crunch beneath my feet and noticed them mixing with the spider-monkey feces cemented to the tread of my boots. The canopy filtered rays of light, guiding my vision to the jungle floor. The ants are a huge part of the jungle environment; in one step I unavoidably crushed armies of them carrying small leaves back to their colony.

This image perfectly illustrated the fragility of the area, a symbol of the relationship of its microcosm to macrocosm. I imagined the scene, hundreds of years ago, when thousands of humans were crushed like these ants by the "foot" of the Spanish army. Tears welled in my eyes.

Apart from a few glyphs, the ancient site of Calakmul bears little evidence of the Snake Dynasty. In fact, most of the records of that dynasty rest at other sites throughout the region. This is how archeologists have pieced together a mere ten percent of what is known about the Kaan: by finding royal tombs and reading the ancient inscriptions on the stelae. These masterpieces were uniquely erected in front of most of the pyramids. Today, due to the regional volatility of its geological material, Mother Nature has eroded the once impressive artwork, making it hard to decipher what was actually written.

It was a bit overwhelming to think of all the work that went into the construction of a stela. I imagined a short, stout man, sitting in the sun, carving away with a chisel at a ten-foot-tall column that weighed a ton. In front of Structure Thirteen is a classic example. I saw a female ruler with a staff of authority.

I believe that this staff energetically represented Kundalini as known by the ancient people of India. To the Maya, the number thirteen represents the feminine. Honoring the feminine was of great importance at Calakmul.

Because the ancient Maya lived in close connection with the cosmos and the earth, they gave great respect to the cycles of life and time. So naturally, since the moon governed their menstrual cycles, women were considered closer to the rhythms of Mother Earth. In this region, females were given more importance in society. These exalted roles were in tune with the natural order of the Creator, as women themselves served as vessels of creation.

Heading along a white road connecting one plaza to another, from Structure Thirteen I eventually came across Structure Thirty-three. In India thirty-three is the number of the serpent, and at Calakmul this structure is known as the "coiled serpent." This also parallels the Vedic writings on Kundalini in the Upanishads, where the subtle serpent energy is depicted as coiled at the base of the spine.

The Vedic tradition from India presents in the Upanishads a series of instructions that teach how to awaken an inner force called Shakti. According to this text, it is the primordial feminine energy that runs through all things in the universe.

All ancient traditions tapped into the same energy that the early Indian people described. This was likely due to the proximity of life to the rhythms of the sun, moon, and stars. I headed to the grand plaza to witness the Kaan glyph. I climbed up the pyramid, and to the top left I saw the record written in stone.

Fig. 2 The Kaan Serpent Glyph
(Image courtesy of *Eli Coberly*)

The next day I headed to Ichkabal, another Mayan site which

predated Calakmul and had ties to the Kaan Dynasty. It means "between lows." Edgar Cayce, dubbed the "sleeping prophet," was a famous conduit for what are called the Akashic records: a repository of all events, thoughts, etc., that have taken place throughout human history. In the 1950s, he once gave a psychic reading to a woman, during which he told her of her past life in Ichkabal. Even though this reading took place some forty years before its discovery in 1995, Cayce, through his clairvoyance, named the city.

The Tourism Board announced that the site would open in 2016, but much more excavation needed to be done first. That year I visited the area. Despite pleading with the local authorities, I was denied entry. Perhaps part of the beauty of human life is to revel in awe of the great mysteries of the universe. But, then again, I thought: why not inquire beyond the known and wade into the waters for greater knowledge?

5

THE CROSS

After that small disappointment, I headed south to Belize to visit Xunantunich. The name means "stone lady"—a Mayan site about eighty miles west of Belize City. The picturesque name is based on reports by visitors over the years of seeing a woman with glowing red eyes, dressed all in white as she ascends the main pyramid at sundown.

That pyramid represents the axis mundi, the rotational axis that connects the earth with the celestial spheres and is located in the center of the city. It features one of the more impressive mural/stucco friezes in all of Mesoamerica. Here you will see where the artist's rendition of the World Tree echoes that of most all global religions.

I was there to see the tomb of a snake king. The excavation was so recent, I thought the archeologists would still be handling the bones or at least a jade necklace. But no dice. Still, I left my heart in Chiapas. I needed to study Palenque again.

In the jungle highlands of Chiapas, Mexico, is a site called

Palenque. It's a relatively recent discovery, which showcases the main Temple of Inscriptions. At the top of the steps is an opening to a passageway leading down two flights, some twenty-five meters, into the center of the pyramid.

In 1952 Alberto Ruiz, a Mexican archeologist, along with his team of local men, rediscovered this hidden gem. They took many years to excavate the overlying limestone rubble, in order to reveal probably the most amazing piece of artwork in Central America: the sarcophagus of the renowned ruler of Palenque, Pakal the Great.

The tomb itself was so heavy, it couldn't be moved. These days tourists are not allowed to view it. Near the ruins is a fully interactive exhibit with a very realistic version of the tomb, explaining the history of this great Mayan ruler. Carved in the limestone is a cross-shaped frieze depicting Pakal himself descending into the underworld. The museum in Palenque displays a quote by Ruiz.

It reads, "At the moment of passing the threshold, I had the strange sensation of penetrating into time at a time that had been stopped a thousand years before." This quote hints at the concept of the cycle of death and rebirth succinct to the Vedic tradition of reincarnation.

Pakal is superimposed on top of the cross and appears to be doing something. There are many speculations as to just what it is he is doing. Some say that he is controlling the instruments of a time machine; others contend there is nothing more to this art than meets the eye.

Pakal's sarcophagus is a stela. In the museum are glyphs that show many illustrations of an ancestral ruling lineage via the family tree. With each ruler representing a kind of fruiting tree, like the cocoa and avocado, and each of these rulers' hands appear to be in a "mudra."

He was given power at the ripe old age of twelve by his mother, Lady Sak K'uk', whose name means "White Quetzal". In another temple is a carving of his mother crowning him as he sits on a double-necked serpent with jaguar heads.

What I continually noticed on my visits were examples of the feminine being of great importance like this in Palenque; it also highlights the powerful combination of the masculine and feminine, and it shows the cyclical nature of the two. The serpent represents the energy path of both sexes, like the Sushumna nadi of the Hatha Yoga tradition. The jaguar heads represent a connection to the cosmos.

Pakal was a ruler of Palenque for many decades. Until his death, he literally shielded his people from neighboring cities with strategic war campaigns against the Kaan. Then his son, Kinich Kan Balam, rose to power and completed the Temple of Inscriptions. Eventually the city declined and was attacked, but not before Kan Balam had erected the most magnificent monument: The Cross Group, a trio of temples that include the Temple of the Sun, the Temple of the Cross, and the Temple of the Foliated Cross.

Located behind the cross group in the sweltering jungle is yet another artistic masterpiece. It's something people often miss when visiting. Partially because most of the time it is off limits due to construction or falling trees and most of the city is unexcavated due to budget and labor limitations. I slipped past the few vendors and witnessed a marvel rarely talked about.

There was Pakal's descendant carved in stone and displayed in the Shoonya mudra. A mudra is defined as a seal where the fingers on the hands are touching each other and certain mudras represent different emotions and elements. The shuni, or Shung, occurs when the middle finger touches the thumb. This is said to represent space and fire. The very two things rooted in the Mayan cosmovision.

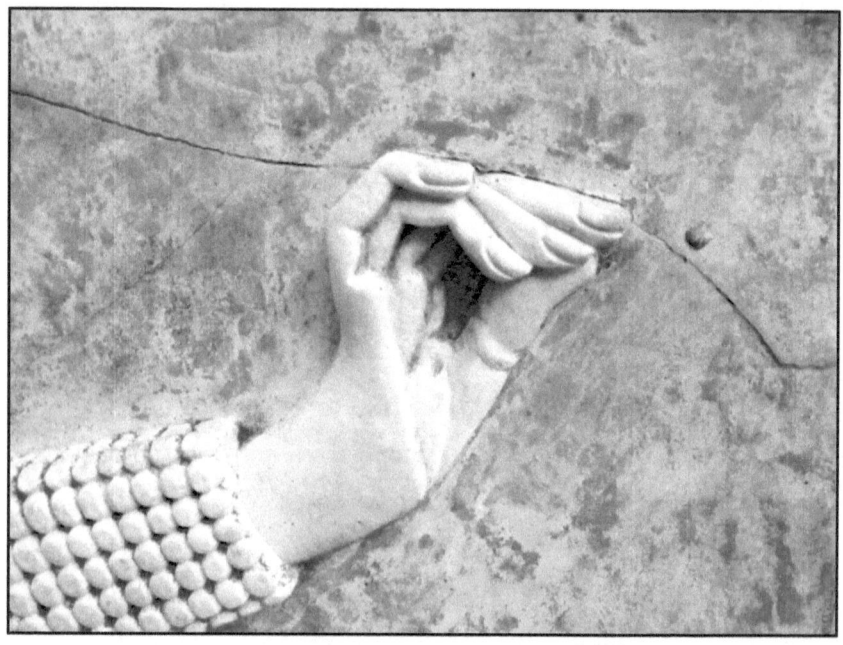

Fig. 3 Mayan mudra on carving of the king K'inich Janaab' Pakal II,
Mayan city of Palenque, Chiapas, Mexico
(Image courtesy of *Eli Coberly*, 2016)

Although the Maya could calculate millions or even billions of years into the future, they show the beginning of time as August 11, 3114 B.C., and the end, as most people know, on December 21, 2012, the winter solstice. It was marked in space and time as a reference to the changing of a new cycle of the earth's axis into the feminine aspect of the larger cycles of the solstices and equinoxes. This is a new opportunity for the world to become conscious of the urgency of our times.

In the center of the cross group of Palenque is a stone altar, probably used for bloodletting of some sort. In 2018, I noticed something when looking over at it from the Temple of the Foliated Cross. If you flew a drone above this centerpiece on the ground, you would see the points of the sri yantra of India.

I have been to Palenque five times and studied it extensively. To me, not only does it have the most unique architecture in all of the land of the Maya, it also bears the most unusual palpable energy. I believe this is due to the massive amounts of water running through its aqueducts, which are the central inner working force behind the city. Electrical conductivity can drastically increase as a result of hydraulics. In Palenque, hydraulic water systems were used to pipe water into the houses of the elite.

The Maya at Palenque were the leading stucco artists of the area. They literally tapped into the source of creation. I have personally examined and studied the cosmological vision illustrated through the stone artwork of this monumental city, and through these eyes I witnessed a culture unique even for the Maya.

It almost seemed that the art and history of a family tree for Palenque was of equal importance to its agriculture. But something else was at play here. There was not only an elaborate story to legitimize the bloodline of its rulership, like one finds in most ancient cities, but a major calculation of time dating back to Predynastic Egypt with a veneration to three gods.

This is an indication of an ability to tell ancestral lineage stories back to the time of creation, which would be hard for anyone to dispute. It was meant to prove to the commoners beyond reasonable doubt that the royal lineage was unchallengeable. And all the creation stories lead to the water.

In today's neo-spiritual movements, or mindfulness communities, you may hear the word "flow" used as slang for a myriad of concepts, in phrases like "How is your flow?" or "That isn't in my flow."

Even Bruce Lee was a proponent of the embodiment of water. While "flow" can be subjective and is often used as a dismissive, irresponsible term for accountability, its true potency involves harnessing the momentum of what is already in motion or in place. This adaptation is a result of generation after generation observing the cycles of the earth, sun, moon, and stars. It might be hard to conceptualize, but once you remove the urgency of time placed on us by colonial agriculture and religion, there is a perfect medium for clairvoyance and connectivity to all that was, is, and will ever be.

6

THE "ATM" CAVE

I n 2017, I arrived in Belize, a popular British-run tourist country, located just east of Guatemala. Its motto is "go slow." The plane touched down at the airport just outside Belize City. When I walked out into the sweltering heat of this Caribbean Sea paradise, I noticed a cool vibration like that of Jamaica. Unlike Jamaica, marijuana isn't legal in Belize. However, this fact was not readily apparent. It seemed that everywhere I looked, I saw Rasta-looking characters smoking big joints.

San Ignacio, just west of Belize City, has been reported as one of the most dangerous cities in the world. To the seasoned traveler it feels just the opposite, unless you're unaccustomed to dogs playing the important role of nightly garbage collectors or to even the occasional catcall. Almost everything is great about this part of the Caribbean, including its beautifully colorful people, its sweet reggae music, and its juicy tropical fruit.

Just down from Main Street is a blocked-off road paved with reddish purple-colored bricks. The street is decorated with cheap floral-printed dresses, tour guide offices, and Coca-Cola umbrellas shading mostly American tourists. A neon sign for the HSBC bank blatantly tells the story of European Colonization: "Our country, your bank." Right across from the bank is a tour guide office where I met a young local man, whose Uncle Gonzo happened to be one of the most knowledgeable cave archeologists in Belize.

Booking a tour of the Actun Tunichil Muknal Cave with Gonzo is a task; he is very popular. Raised in the Cayo District, he is a man of the people, and he believes not only in preserving the local flora and fauna but also the tradition of the Maya. A family man, Gonzo stands about five and a half feet tall, with a muscular build and a gleam in his eyes. At times the gleam gives way to a gaze that encompasses the masculinity of a warrior. He sports a messed-up hairdo and a salt-and-pepper beard.

He was one of the original members of the exploration of the "ATM" Cave under the supervision of expert Dr. Jaime Awe. For Gonzo, cave navigation is second nature. It has been since the days of his barefooted youth. He is well aware of the follies of quick archeological conclusions in the name of fame. For him, it's personal, because his family lineage has practiced their way of life here for thousands of years.

Gonzo does little guide work and is selective with his clientele. Most of his time is spent looking after other sites and developing sustainable tourism practices. When he does guide, though, he provides a world-class experience.

We entered the cave the following day, where he reunited with an old college buddy, who went by the name of King Kong. Kong, a Chinese-American archeologist, had lived for a decade in San

Ignacio and was back for the first time in many years. He was accompanied by two of his students, Lucy and Muchen. They were smart, young Asian-American women, already asking questions about everything under the sun, moon, and stars. I felt like I'd won the adventure-buddy lottery.

The ATM Cave system is over an hour's drive from the city, through agricultural countryside surrounded by miles of jungle. We drove through many water crossings and arrived in the parking lot, the scent of orange blossoms wafting sweet surrender. I was ready to enter the underworld of the Maya.

Gonzo took us on a journey, not an adventure. Over the next kilometer we crossed the river three times on foot. He wanted to be sure that we were aware of the sacredness of this cave to the Maya people.

When I asked him about the Mayan connection to the feminine, he replied, "The cave, to the Maya, is sacred. Just as one should show respect for a womb, you must ask permission to enter." The Mayan tradition was to tender offerings at the mouth of the cave; if they felt the gods refused their offering, they would turn back. I imagined all sources of the secrets of life and death being respected with such reverence.

After we entered by diving into the crystal blue water, which flowed from the mouth of this seven-kilometer cave system, it became very dark. We turned on our headlamps, illuminating the presence of stalactites formed by water dripping from the ceiling. The cave had a few tight squeezes, offering just enough room for a small-framed person, but then often opened into fifty-by-fifty-foot chambers with formations on all sides. Further exploration revealed thousands of sparkling, chandelier-like formations. Deeper in the crystal cave are relics, which tell a story of death and what it meant to the elite ruling class of the Maya.

The scattered human skeletal remains have helped archeologists piece together an explanation for the sacrifices that appeased the rain god, Chaac. Lying on the cavern floor were the finger, rib, and femur bones of children. There was also the occasional adult skull, and many clay pots. The pots, red in color, ranged in size and were used for ceremonial purposes.

Bloodletting was a sacred ritual to appease the gods. When a massive drought hit the Central American region in the Late Classic Period, the priests and priestesses went deeper into the caves of Xibalba, the underworld. There they offered to the gods the blood of the people, so that they could receive water for the essence of life: maize. Crop failure was a huge problem at that time, and to the Maya the solution was human sacrifice.

Ixchel, the goddess of the moon and healing, played a big role in the development of feminine wisdom and practices. The Maya cherished the concept that the closer they approached the embodiment of the goddess, the closer they would come to fertility: the life force of the Maya. They thought that, if they went with reverence to the source of water, which they believed was the source of creation, the goddess would grant them a fluidity of the universe that would further their elite bloodline.

About halfway to our destination, there was something I was lucky to see. It was something most tours never catch a glimpse of. After climbing a slippery limestone cliff, we found what appeared to be an ancient offering.

Gonzo exclaimed, "Here it is!"

"Here what is?" asked the students in unison.

"Perhaps the only cave stela found in all of Mesoamerica," he answered. "Two giant-shaped Clovis spear points, with a pot and a figurine. A sort of monument to Ixchel, the Mayan goddess."

"After the pots were used, a piece from each was removed, or they were smashed entirely," Gonzo explained.

The students asked, "Why?"

"Sometimes in termination of a time period or ritual sacrifice for rain," Kong explained.

We traversed farther over boulders, fitting through tight squeezes and wading through deep pools. Approximately one and a half kilometers back, we observed a face-down entire skeleton covered in crystalline limestone. Contrary to popular belief (and the advertisements of all the tour companies), the skeleton was that of a seventeen-year-old male, not that of a woman. For some reason, a young maiden's skeleton is considered more shocking to view than a man's.

This young man's midsection was chopped in half, and he'd been disemboweled.

This cave revealed a violent past in a culture rooted in ritual sacrifice. The ancient Maya believed in the sacrifice of a few for the greater good of the elite ruling class. Sound familiar?

Why were the Maya labeled as savages when in our own culture war has manifested in hideous forms? Why should one God or religion or form of prayer be superior to any other when most prayers arise from an interest in furthering your kin.

War has been a staple since the need to create borders of

property; and this war was for agriculture. When entire societies attempted to play God with Mother Nature, power arose. This power was needed to control the population and to preserve and continue the advancements in agriculture.

In ancient times, as in other cultures, Maya men discovered that the fruit of their labor could produce more food. More food meant healthier children and more deforestation of the jungle to create more stucco. In this model we see a ruler feeling the need to be responsible for an entire group. But for the Maya, when the climate changed or crops failed, suddenly there was a need to ask "why?" of a Higher Power.

In the beginning of agriculture, women played a large role in the fertility ritual. Men knew that there was great wisdom hidden in the moment when their seed united with an egg. Here was an energetic connection and a reason to worship a Higher Power. But things got sticky when men saw control begin to slip through their fingers.

War was born in the hearts of men when agriculture and the extraction of resources became secondary to survival. Rulers became accustomed to a lifestyle in which they stood in the center of things, replacing Mother Nature. Even today we see a laundry list of men who didn't achieve enough or didn't provide enough for their families.

This idea of lack shattered the temporary illusion of integrity. We have been taught that, if one doesn't control an outcome, one isn't successful. This just isn't the case. In fact, reality is the complete opposite—replacing fear with love begets timelessness.

Women have always shared a special message of that which is

whispered on the wind. It is in the heart that miracles happen. We create, every second of every day. What are you creating at this moment in your heart? Is it war or love? Mayan women commonly possessed the status to perform elaborate rituals, and they even ruled in some cases. The descendants of these powerful women from ancient times still exist today.

But they aren't performing bloodletting. Instead, they connect with the cycles and rhythms of the mother goddess, Ixchel. Wishing to connect the dots to a lineage, I asked Gonzo where I could find a practicing female with tradition of the old ways. He offered to point me in the right direction.

On the way to the ATM Cave is the home of a woman named Maria. She and her mother represent a lineage of healers which embody the goddess. In Mayan art, that goddess is depicted with bare breasts, holding a water lily, and on her head is a serpent.

I asked Maria for an interview. She looked to be about fifty years young, and in her eyes I saw a darkness I felt I could trust. She said, "I will give you an interview, but in order to truly understand the connection of my lineage you must take part in our sacrament."

The process involved eating seeds from a flower she called Lol-K'in, which in Mayan means "flower of the sun." This white flower with several petals grows in a bunch of twenty-two, and the seeds are harvested right in time for the traditional equinox ceremony, which occurs around the twentieth of March.

Three years prior to this, I received in meditation a vision of a five-petaled white flower. Then I beheld a map with a pinpoint highlighted in northwestern Guatemala. At the time I had never been to Guatemala and had no knowledge of the flora and fauna in its jungle. I stored the experience of my encounter with Maria in the back of my mind.

I ingested the Lol-K'in seeds at midnight, and the goddess ceremony lasted until noon. That way, half of my experience took place at night in darkness and half in the light of day. Maria claimed that the Lol-K'in flower was unique to her family lineage, explaining that this was how the Maya got all their codices, stelae, artwork, and even the cosmological vision.

I asked her, "Is this for real?"

"For us this ceremony offers a period of renewal; afterward, following a period of rest. That is the time for bringing one's cosmological vision into the world," she explained. "The seeds are bearers of artistic vision. When you hold these seeds next to your heart and ask for guidance, you will receive what's needed for healing. Think about this, and whether you are ready to receive the vision, while I cook my lunch."

I sat in her gift shop full of ancient depictions of deities and scenes found at pyramids that she had carved in slate. Looking at the small museum filled with antiquities from her ancestors, my head began to swim with questions.

It appeared to me then that perhaps it wasn't in the cards for me to touch anything even resembling an entheogen. I had made it my life's work to learn about the Mayan Cosmo-Vision. With bated breath I sat in contemplation, wondering what the noble path forward might be.

Here I was at yet another crossroads, with an opportunity to learn from the pure lineage of the Itzamna society. I had sought answers and instead found myself tripping on a metaphorical game of psychedelic rock, paper, and scissors. I concluded that a decision must have been made long before I walked through the museum door.

Soon Maria returned. I told her I was ready. She led me out back to a small room where she burned copal (tree resin) incense, telling me that the sap of the Ceiba tree was sacred. "It is believed that the Ceiba is the World Tree that embodies the great time-cycle of life and death."

Moments later, she handed me twenty-two seeds. I ate them without hesitation. Taking a deep breath, I gazed through smoke-induced visions, receiving wondrous glimpses into my subconscious.

The seeds induced a sleepy feeling, while dark shadows in my mind danced with an interdimensional white light, flooding my vision in an experience similar to a Kundalini yoga awakening.

Out of all the psychedelics one can ingest, this one virtually stops time. Eight hours passed in what felt like ten minutes. Throughout the process, Maria brought in herbs and tobacco mixed with copal, which produced a very pungent aroma. The effects lasted for eight to ten hours, much like LSD, but these seeds brought me to a place in the eternal now that echoed a concept of José Argüelles—"Time is art."

I recognized this art as the timeless place of conception between the mother and father. It was a potent renaissance of the masculine and feminine, in which I envisioned a parallel concept of the Sri Yantra, the mystical diagram of the Vedic tradition.

Eventually, at dark, the ceremony ended. I fired up my rental car and drove back to the city. That day Maria helped me to realize just how much psychedelics played a role in Mayan society. I needed to see more, I needed to follow the roots of the flower.

7

THE TREE OF LIFE

There are those who say that everything happens for a reason and that there is a divine intelligent order behind all life. Many of us search for truth and meaning through religion and philosophy, attempting to glean the purpose of our limited time on earth. Another route is that of renouncing all views of a Higher Power and an afterlife. I myself lean toward neutrality when it comes to unearthing the mystery of the unknown.

Fear of death has been a theme throughout recorded history. We place importance on controlling the uncontrollable, achieving the unachievable, and pushing through evolution with a self-inflated sense of importance. Upon our deathbeds most of us regret working too hard, not loving enough, and not forgiving others. What we end up with is dissatisfaction over many of our personal choices. Why can't we be satisfied in the end with the comfort of knowing that our lessons will continue?

Something like two people die every second on this earth, around fifty-five million each year. It is the one thing that we know will happen to all of us, sooner or later. Death is what we wait for all our lives, yet when it comes knocking, we often act surprised.

Most of the indigenous peoples throughout the world and its history have always viewed death as a single step along the long path of the continuation of the soul. In the West we seem to see it as an end, so we grasp and cling to familiarity, hoping for comfort in something that is about to expire. This expiration is ephemeral life as we know it, but that doesn't mean our souls will not go on— at least, according to many ancient indigenous cultures.

So we search for immortality by prolonging our lives with new health products, and breakthroughs in medical technologies and science, only to realize that we all must still complete the great cycle of life as we know it. The physical body is of no use in the afterlife; yet, in most cultures, humans try to bring the body and the soul with them.

In the US alone more than thirty thousand heart surgeries are performed each year, with about a 50 percent success rate. In Russia there is a company called 3D Bio Printing Solutions that prints organs. Only, there's a catch. While they might be able to hook these organs up, there are certain limitations. The actual biological nuances cannot yet be replicated. It appears that humans are missing a key point. After all, a perfect medium for healing and cellular reproduction exists in Mother Nature. Still, despite our interest in prolonging life, there remains a need for faith.

There are those who believe that heaven exists right here on earth. This furthers the idea that the soul carries on; like the waves on the ocean, everything has its cycles and purpose. Within most major religions, or worldviews, we find some type of belief in the Tree of Life.

Knowledge of the Tree has been gleaned from a nearly forgotten past that was by and large destroyed in the major conquests of history.

The victors destroyed the victims' cultures by murdering, raping, and whipping their people into submission. Violence is deeply rooted in the subconscious and has perpetuated itself in our relationships since well before the immaculate conception of Jesus through the Virgin Mary.

When Jesus was born, the Magi came from the East, bearing gifts of Frankincense, Gold, and Myrrh. They were from the Zoroastrian religion, descendants of an ancient Persian ruler named Darius the Great. Zoroastrians worshiped the fire of creation. Through the one God Creator, they became masters of energy and magic.

If similar earth-based societies all believed in a journey of the soul, how did that teaching become so standardized? What did the ancients know, and how did they know it? What can we learn from them that will help humans survive the atrocities of war, hatred, and the abuse of Mother Earth?

There is now in progress a retrofit of not only what it means to be a man, but also what masculinity means. People are waking from the slumber of outdated belief systems imposed by a warlike patriarchal agenda. Herein lies not only an opportunity for change, but also one for balance. As an intelligent species, it is up to us to not make the same errors of the past as we speed ahead into a future that many see as bleak.

One path of transformation can take place through the intake of ayahuasca, the plant medicine of the Amazon in Peru. Ayahuasca is a combination of a vine *Banisteriopsis caapi* and the leaves of the chacruna plant from the Amazon jungle. When you ingest one without the other, nothing pharmaceutical happens. But together the MAOI inhibitor hits the stomach and floods the brain barrier for a spiked serotonin overload causing dizziness, vomiting, and life-changing, integrity-checking hallucinations.

The above-mentioned is a vehicle that works for many, but not for all. You will see in Los Angeles what appears to be an unlimited number of yoga teachers, business coaches, self-help gurus, goddess warrior-woman types, and tantric teachers. Many of them lack life experience, teaching credentials, personal knowledge, or original opinions. Yet somehow the fraudulent among them are successful as they lead the blind to the slaughter of individual discernment.

In this hypothetical spiritual smorgasbord, you will hear the same buzzwords: "empowerment, letting go, trusting, safe containers, self-care, inner work, wild women, priestess, and goddess." What a beautiful and encouraging perpetuation of evolution. Yet the shadow side of it all is that many teachers, who have taken on this role, do it mostly for financial gain, popularity, and/or validation. Many of these folks aren't really teachers; they are more like social-media influencers.

If we examine the roots of this situation, you will often see abuse that occurred when someone was a child, well-off busy families that ignored the needs of the child, and perhaps a need to belong somewhere other than in a rigid social or oppressive religious structure. Traumatically influenced souls who seek change and a sense of belonging often find gurus in the Los

Angeles area with minimal experience in serving the potent hallucinogenic beverage of the jungle mentioned earlier.

When the weekend seminar is over, the participants are dumped off in the city to fend for themselves, providing them a tough medium in which to integrate what many deem as a deep, life-changing experience. The problem lies not so much in that a chemical dependency has been initiated, but that an addiction to serotonin is perpetuated.

This creates an advanced inquiry like that which arises from many years of meditation or psychotherapy. As with any practice of radical self-improvement, integration must occur or nothing will change, and the practice becomes nothing more than another party.

Prescription drugs for depression and similar symptoms are becoming an epidemic, and people will look anywhere to treat the symptom, but almost never at the root cause. So, when many people find Ayahuasca, they look to it as a blanket-fix for all of their problems. If you come across anyone or any group that claims that their medicine is a cure-all, run as fast as you can in the opposite direction. It is certainly a master plant teacher, and it is one formula for rapid transformation, but it is not "the alpha and the omega."

So many Amazon shamans and plastic cowboy shamans of the United States dole it out at two hundred dollars a night for a weekend or up to two weeks. Many of the people who come to these shamans are at the end of their rope, without knowledge of their bodies, their allergies, or contraindications to the medicine. There are true stories of more than a few radical physical healings, but mostly emotional and psychological ones. A small fraction of historical accounts tell a story of death, rape, psychotic episodes, and even worsening conditions than those known prior to ingestion.

As this method for transformation rapidly grows in popularity, studies are underway to illuminate its benefits and drawbacks. I conclude that not all participants are wired with a proper conductivity to handle such a shock to their systems. Without a medical contingency to do an extensive workup of the body, you are playing a form of Russian roulette. If you believe in the immortality of the soul, then you are good to go, because ayahuasca, like many other drugs, increases the heart rate.

So the Western contingency of spiritual seekers will continue to compound their trauma with additional traumas. The cleverly disguised, tight container bolsters the dogma that is disguised as nondogma, while the critical self-made thinkers remain ostracized as they speak up to unjust, cult-like, spiritual-bypass behavior.

Trauma remains a playground for the addict of serotonin. It is a perfect mask for those who wish to hide in a container of safety, preventing them from dealing with the root cause of their cycles. Spiraling out of control, the self-made coaches give out a panacea of cookie-cutter advice to anyone willing to listen. They use sexuality on social media to attract customers, and then complain about all the unwanted sexual advances they attract as a result.

Women, the guardians of the gateway to the future of our planet, are now stepping up in a powerful way. They are creating safe spaces for expression without fear or judgment. You can see the perpetuation of the opposite through hatred toward men or anything masculine. While the anger is justified, the hatred is not.

It is what I call "reverse-shaming." Because of their pain, they want to drag others into the void of negativity.

Of course, this process is not limited to women, but for now I am speaking of the feminine. Yes, women have been over-sexualized, but women do the same thing to men. No, it hasn't been equal, but there will never be change if hatred is directed at half the population for being the people they were born and raised to be.

Within both men and women, you will see the energy of masculine and feminine qualities expressing themselves. The media's exposure of racism, sexism, and classism is a step in the right direction. Yet, there is still too much division. Women want equality, period. It is time we give them just that. However, this doesn't include placating them, nor bowing down to them in fear. It takes development and a harmonious blending of masculine and feminine qualities within oneself to lead to a greater understanding of the self.

8

In November 2017, I took a trip to Mexico while en route to Peru to study not only the Mormon connection in Central America and the Tree of Life, but also the possibility of DNA modification in the desert of South America. I was on my way to the site of Izapa, in Tapachula, a town in the state of Chiapas, Mexico. This location predated the Maya, although the indigenous people were eventually assimilated into the Mayan culture.

The first people here were the Olmec, whose signature stone-work were eight-ton heads found on the west side of the Isthmus, with similar facial features to the people of Africa. There has been speculation that these people were descendants of African tribes.

Olmec origins are hard to prove since the Spanish destroyed the records of Olmec history. Maybe a discovery is on the horizon about the trade routes of ancient peoples and how those routes affected the consciousness of their religions. For now, the history stands as "his-story", accounts of the elite male rulers who dominated the region.

I arrived with a sore throat and a bad Spanish vocabulary, the latter a symptom I seem to come down with every time I visit Mesoamerica. To be honest, sometimes I feel like a stranger in a real estate market accessing the probability of my speculation. What makes it more of a challenge is piecing together answers to the questions I have. The local population seems to either not give a shit or just wants my money. All in all, I encounter no danger in Central America. The people are as warm as the weather.

The region, hot and dry, is where cacao has been cultivated for thousands of years, thanks to the perfect combination of an ideal climate and rich mineral deposits. A smoldering volcano off in the distance towered over these relatively small ruins. I imagined that its fiery lava was to thank for such fertility.

When the taxi dropped me off, the air was sticky and the Izapa site was filled with Catholic-uniform-wearing, gawking teenagers more interested in taking selfies than in the history of their ancestors. The grass growing around the ruins was freshly cut, as it otherwise provided the perfect hiding place for many piles of ground-up dog shit. I narrowly avoided these unpleasant surprises as I strolled through the ruins. I had a one-track mind as I now held a question in my head in Spanish. "*¿Donde esta Arbor de la Viva?*"

As I alluded to earlier, a stela is a Mayan stone carving that depicts a story. It is essentially a class of hieroglyph. At most Mayan sites you pay an entry fee and an attendant signs you in and gives you a ticket. I asked the attendant where to find the Tree of Life, and he pointed me down the street. There I came across an old man wielding a machete. He grinned at me, revealing a few gold teeth.

The old man informed me that I had nearly reached my goal,

and so I continued, soaked in sweat, and noticed a road made of cobblestone. I followed it toward the archeological site. Sadly, I observed rotting cacao beans nearby being eaten by birds. In an agrarian society where you have a surplus of what isn't a commodity elsewhere in the world, you'll see such products wasted locally. I thought that a comparison could be made, and a lesson learned: cacao is to Izapa what "Mary Jane" is to Northern California.

I found the entrance I sought and began to take notice of all the barely readable stelae of this ancient culture. Izapa was a ceremonial site intrinsically designed to educate people about the creation story of the Maya. All the carvings were specific to the journey of the soul into Xibalba, the underworld. On most of the carvings one sees a serpent, which represents the journey of feminine energy, as well as a story of a voyage in a canoe in the water of the underworld.

Also, the Hero Twins, who represent the sun and moon, are teaching the concept of union for creation. This is the essence of the Mayan creation story. This union of the masculine and feminine brings sustenance of the life-force energy in the form of maize or corn.

How were the energy-based concepts of the Maya people and those of the Hindus of the East linked? In Sanskrit the word Akasha means "ether." In that case, how did the Maya echo a concept of energy from a civilization on the other side of the world, and of a different time period? Did they travel to other civilizations? Or did those other civilizations travel to them? Perhaps they linked through their subconscious meditations.

As I pondered this question, out of nowhere came a few hundred of those teenagers, demanding selfies with me for Facebook. So, I obliged and moved on. After strolling through many more cacao forests, I saw the road gave way to a clearing. And there stood the sacred stone of Izapa, depicting none other than the Tree of Life.

Now a weathered carving and barely visible to the human eye, this stone shows a tree with many elves (or people wearing pointy hats), performing a ritual under a large tree. At the base of the tree carved in stone are people situated on a boat in the underworld, making a connection to their creation story. This creation is born of combining Mother Earth and Father Sky. The mother represents the moon goddess, Ixchel, and the father, Izamna, is a lizard.

What would a moon goddess and a lizard have to do with creation?

The Maya were great masters of time. It was through tracking and recording celestial events that they were able to farm better, forecast weather patterns, and even predict the arrival of visitors from foreign lands. They recognized that rare occurrences in the sky prefaced rare occurrences on earth; it was a mirror of heaven on earth. They proved this to be true through their unique calendar, foretelling the arrival of many alleged incarnations of Kukulkán, Gugumatz, or Quetzalcoatl, the Lizard Sky God.

There is no scientific way to prove the existence of such a being, but one can extrapolate a Joseph Campbell-like perspective, where everything is manifesting over time through symbolism, and more specifically, in indigenous culture through animism. It was through the embodiment of the characteristics of animals during psychedelic rituals that people learned the concept of transfor-mation. We see the same cyclical depictions of God and Goddess through all forms of religion in an effort to encapsulate the human experience into the afterlife.

The Mayan calendar heralded a connection to time and space lacking in its Gregorian counterpart. It is through the realization of this connection that one can recognize the divinity of creation in the present moment, where our perceived ideas blend with the cosmos and melt into the sea of primordial awareness of unity.

Yet, how can one recognize these markers for transformation? The answer is that we must revel in synchronicity.

Fig. 4 Drawing, Izapa, Mexico, Stela Five
(Image by *Madman2001* via Wikipedia)

9

PERU

It was November 11, 2017. Five years had passed since I'd first decided to dive into the intuitive abyss and follow synchronicity. I disembarked from my plane and hailed a cab to the nearest Chifa (Chinese-Peruvian food) restaurant. While seating myself I noticed a man in ragged clothes outside, sporting a pan flute. He made a beeline into the restaurant where he played for me a perfect rendition of "Dust in the Wind," a song by Kansas that transported me to a memory about seven years prior.

The year was 2010, I was in Peru, and at that time I was married. My wife and I had decided to visit several temples outside of Lima. We were on a pyramid overlooking the city, holding hands and walking.

Back in the third grade a teacher asked the class to draw pictures of us in the future. I drew one of me with lots of tattoos, like I have now, and clasping the hand of a woman in what seemed to be a faraway country. Many years later I looked over at her and remembered that crude pencil sketch I had made of us. We continued and I never said a word, though all the hair on my arm stood on end as if each could sense the powerful feeling of that déjà vu.

The plan had been for my wife and me to visit the Nazca Lines, a place on the southern coast where you can see the outlines of animals and geometric shapes carved into the desert sand if you soar overhead in a Cessna. Some say aliens carved these ancient works of art; others hypothesize that the indigenous people created them as a form of communication with extraterrestrials. The rest believe they were built to gain knowledge of the stars, to ensure successful crops.

We arrived in the town of Pisco and hired a plane to fly us over the desert the following day. It was wine country and harvest time. Pisco is world famous for its sours—stiff drinks made from grapas, the distilled liquor of grapes. We pulled over and checked into a dusty, vine-covered hacienda made of old yellow bricks.

A man who looked to be about eighty informed us that he had just made a fresh batch of liquor. He asked if we would like to try some while he demonstrated the process. He didn't have to twist my arm; at the time I was an avid drinker, always looking forward to my next buzz.

We pulled up chairs next to a purple bougainvillea that surrounded the distillery and enjoyed the view of a nearby pheasant on a leash. Then he served us the clear liquid. We clinked our glasses, and I'll be damned if that stuff didn't burn my throat like the nine levels of hell, with each moment burning hotter than the last.

Five hours later we were singing songs with a Peruvian brother and sister from New York who enjoyed dual citizenship. The brother was unwilling to say just what he did in the Big Apple, but his sister had a business making diamond-encrusted and -plated gold-bullet pendants. The bullets screwed open, she explained, and held anything up to two grams. I assumed they ran a family cocaine business, but I was too polite to ask.

A few hours after that I was starting to see triple. The young woman demanded in her sexiest Hispanic voice to the awkward middle-aged waiter, "Come, give us some food to soak up the alcohol." I asked for the third time that she let us go to bed and, finally, we stumbled back to our room, playing bumper cars with a few chairs and plants along the way. We tripped into our spinning bed and passed out.

Several hours later I awoke with my head hanging off the bottom of the bed, facing the television. I decided to switch it on, and to my surprise I saw a wrecked Cessna in the desert of Nazca with only a tail sticking out of the rubble. The tail had the same numbers as the plane we were supposed to board. To this day I'm not sure if there was a lesson in all this, but I sure was happy we had decided to drink those Pisco sours.

The next day we headed to the coast to see the Humboldt penguins, unaware that a tsunami was fast approaching South America, by way of Japan. By the time we arrived in a cab, all the people had gathered on top of the buildings and were warning us to turn around. So, I yelled to the cabbie, "¡Vamanos! ¡Rapido!" and we chirped out. As we headed down the highway, we decided to proceed to Cusco, Peru, and then to Machu Picchu.

However, as if all that we'd experienced wasn't enough, we

noticed something on the news in a bus station. Cusco was flooded, and the Incan trail to Machu Picchu had become impassable. We waited a day or so in a hostel, but it turned out that the Cusco flooding was so intense, it caused the deceased locals to float down the roads. The cemetery caretakers interred their dead above ground.

When the water subsided, hundreds of corpses littered the street, making an easy meal for the many feral dogs. A plane crash, a tsunami, and some rabid corpse-eating dogs later, we decided to head north to the ruins of Caral.

This ancient site, about five thousand years old, is famous for its peaceful inhabitants, who incorporated spirals into their architecture. We took a twelve-hour bus ride and two hours in a *collectivo*—a small van packed full of people. We were the last passengers dropped at the end of the line in a tiny town next to a massive cornfield.

I noticed a few bald chickens pecking at the ground. One was dining out of a potato chip bag. Past the chickens was the only *tienda* (shop) in town. We walked in and asked the clerk, pestered by flies buzzing around his sweaty face, where Caral was. He conferred with someone in the back of the shop and told us that he and his son would take us on mules to see the ruins.

We jumped on donkeys that wore blankets for saddles and ropes for halters. They led us about three kilometers through a cornfield, and then across a river to the driest, most barren desert I had ever seen. Rugged mountains framed the center of a desert canyon, revealing ruins still being excavated from the ancient sand. On top of each pyramid, in the center, were spirals—just as we had been promised by our trusty *Lonely Planet* guidebook.

The ruins of Caral predated predynastic Egypt. It was a peaceful city. In the brief tour, I saw an illustration board explaining the 32 flutes that provided seven tones for undertone resonance. Many of these same tones were outlawed by the Roman Catholic Church. The flutes were used for healing.

Used in conjunction was the *quipu*, a stringed device that looked like something you might find on a young woman's Bohemian Pinterest board. Only this was a record keeper of sorts with beads that could be found around the world.

Used for trading, the written history tells a story of harmonic resonance based on color spectrum and tone. It was used mathematically and tonally the same language of the sri yantra, the holy device of India and referenced in the Vedas.

In Vedic history there was an ancient concept of animism, the circle of animals. It came by way of Sumeria, harkening back to the Epic of Gilgamesh.

This circle of animals eventually became the circle of the Zodiacs. All of this can be traced back to the original circle of animals in Göbekli Tepe in Turkey. This ancient site, as old as twelve thousand years, is the first example of religion and the first instance of animism through harmonic resonance.

This experience left a lasting impression about time and rhythm, how its concepts weren't limited to geography or specific settlements. It was the first time I had experienced exchanging valued things I'd been expecting for something unexpected and better . . . something greater.

I thought I could live this way, following one synchronistic event to the next in search of the mysteriously satisfying unknown. It took seven years and nearly sixty visits to different sacred Mesoamerican sites before my life changed in the way I had imagined. With this reflection of the past in mind, I was grateful to be arriving in Cusco.

10

SERPENT WIS-DUMB

C usco, Peru, is a gem of a city. At night the center's colonial Catholic Church towers over a twinkling courtyard replete with vendors, and even a McDonald's tucked away in a corner. Adjacent to that, stand a couple of museums, sandwiched between three overflowing porta-potties leaking fluid far down the cobblestone street.

First world countries usually don't have this problem. I always feel blessed, when I arrive home from a trip, not having to smell urine or feces every few hundred feet.

Just within a stone's throw of the heart of Cusco are half a dozen or more well-advertised ayahuasca retreat offices. I am an advocate of "opening sacred doors," but from what I witnessed, the doors were closed.

Well, I suppose, as they say, "nothing is sacred." There is a real need to redefine what "sacred" means.

Sometimes in yoga or in New Age communities, you'll hear the word "container" used in situations beyond the obvious. For those unfamiliar with this alternative meaning of the word container, it refers to a particular environment—usually the emotional space provided by a healer or shaman so that someone may explore or deal with trauma, i.e. open up emotionally and feel safe to do so.

Whether through a tantric workshop or a psychoactive life-changing experience, the term "container" has been converted into the likes of a cheap hooker on meth yearning for another fix. Or, better yet, a Nigerian spambot on Craigslist phishing you to send a Western Union money order. Most of us can do better with some white sage and a beat-up copy of the Yoga Sutras. I sometimes think I should invent a container for the "container" that would capture all the leaky behavior that spills like Budweiser at a Super Bowl game.

I decided to investigate, to see if my judgments were accurate. When I walked into one of those places, the one with the best signage out front, I was met by a very friendly local man. I could tell that he had a background in hustling potentially interested clients, which can lend good to any business. I told him I wanted information on what they were doing and that I was writing a book. He invited me up a creaky set of wooden stairs. The wall was plastered with Shipibo textiles, a representation of the *Icaros* (songs) of the jungle.

I entered the waiting room for would-be participants. A few people were milling around and three were seated. As I sat down, I noticed my liaison talking to a man in an Adidas sweatsuit. He whispered in his ear in Spanish, seemingly asking whether I could have a short interview.

The pimp-looking gentlemen asked, "To what purpose?" without a smile or a glance at me. The man told him I was writing a book. He acted put out by my inquiry as he flipped through a big stack of US hundred-dollar bills. Then the liaison ushered me upstairs where he informed me that I had to pay a donation. I told him this might be possible and asked how much he needed. He refused to tell me, so I refused to give a donation.

I could see that this man had bastardized a timeless tradition. The guy in the Adidas sweatsuit was like any other middleman. He was in the biz to make as much money on both ends as possible. As far as I could tell, he had no interest in offering a personal, sacred experience.

I left to explore a few other places. At this point it was getting late and all the retreat offices were closed. What I did see were signs saying, "Ayahuasca ceremony every day at 7 p.m.," and "The Shaman Shop." Ayahuasca is a door and it can often be one that opens more rapidly than most have bargained for.

If you were planning to drive a Ferrari on a windy highway to another dimension of heaven and hell, wouldn't you want someone in the passenger seat asking you how you were doing? When your foot turns to mush and falls through the floor into a fiery lake of your shame and pain, wouldn't you want a friend to help you bring your foot back up through the floorboard?

If you answered no to that question, then go ahead and treat the sacred like a bitch. If you have a need to take a psychoactive drug for recreation, try LSD or mushrooms. You'll be much happier that you did. Would you consult a doctor without a referral? This is your life, emotional health, and body. If you are going to try ayahuasca, do so in a remote safe space through the referral of a longtime friend and in the hands of a professional or reputable shaman.

Towering over Cusco is a site called Saqsayhuaman. I spoke with a local woman about its history, and she said to me, "When the Spaniards found Cusco, they sacked it in less than an hour and moved on to sublimate the priests. After the battle, the Andean people were captured, and the Spanish did the unthinkable, using their sacred temples for jail cells. What was once used for a connection to Mother Earth became a daily reminder for the people of their defeat."

If you talk to the local people about whether one should refer to them as Incan, you will get an answer that you might not expect. They say that their king was Incan, but the people were Andean. More than that, they state that the country of Peru at the time of conquest was divided into four regions and an Incan king ruled over each.

Fig. 5 The Chakana, Inca Symbol
(*ARTYchoke Designs* via Shutterstock.com)

I knew that prior to the trip, the *chakana* (or Incan cross) is a stepped cross. It is made up of an equal-armed cross, indicating the cardinal points of the compass, and a superimposed square. It was much like the Mayan World Tree, in that it represented the trinity of the underworld, earth, and heaven—except an animal was assigned to represent each of those realms.

In the underworld was the serpent, on the earth was the puma, and in the heavens was the condor. It was the shaman who provided a journey through the hole in the center of the cross. This hole represented the axis mundi, as in the Mayan concept. The route of the serpent, if you will. The shamans used many different techniques to aid in this transit, many of which involved plants or their derivatives.

Some forty minutes by taxi from Pisac, also known as the Sacred Valley, these practices are still in use today. Over the years the word has spread about this Peruvian valley, and several tourists began to show up back in their respective countries with tales of visions, transformations, and purges of their psyche.

This exposure provided an opportunity for an upgrade of the collective DNA. Since then, a genuine emergence of healers has risen to the "upgrade challenge." The dark side is there are many gringo pseudo-shamans using these mind-altering substances for personal gain. I began to ask questions to get to know the foreigners who seemed to outnumber the locals.

Diving into the culture, I met several *kambo* practitioners, some claiming to be shamans and others just holding ceremonies for a quick buck. *Kambo* is venom from a toad; it's used to remove toxins from the organs and bloodstream. I noticed that the hotel I was staying in was swimming with these practitioners. It felt like I had walked into a den of newly certified two-hundred-an-hour yoga teachers. Everyone was excited about what kambo had done for him or her.

I opted out of all the ceremonies, citing high blood pressure from the last Amazonian medicine I had ingested. As the days progressed, I noticed that most of the travelers in the hotel were snorting rapé, a powerful Peruvian snuff. One day out front I spotted a young Eastern European named Yuri, wearing baggy Thai pants and sporting a man bun. Draped over him was an even younger French girl. He was doling out the snuff like it was her allowance. Sitting on his lap, she begged for more every minute. For them this was perhaps a practice of letting go, but I saw in this episode yet another bastardization of tradition.

Later, at midnight, a man asked for Yuri at the front desk. "I need a vacuum sealer for the shipment," he explained. I confirmed with the man that this hotel had branched out into shipping the cosmic snuff around the world to people who wanted a religious experience. It seemed like a decent thing, spreading medicine to the world. But I remembered that snuff stops the pituitary gland from secreting, which ultimately blocks the thyroid from doing its job. This further confirmed my suspicion that moderation with substances is an important discipline that helps people to perpetuate the sacred.

11

WHO'S THE ALIEN NOW?

T hrough the center of the Sacred Valley runs the Vilcanota River, where a bridge gives access to a small town of streets made of stone. Perched two kilometers above the town are masterfully built ruins with a view of the entire valley. There are a lot of theories floating around the proverbial ether about who handled the construction.

Some of the blocks are small and of crude construction. While others are larger.

The larger ones have joints that indicate more advanced masonry. There are many archeologists and New Age types, who believe that there is no logical explanation for how the larger blocks were moved from their original quarry, which is positioned more than a few kilometers on the other side of the expansive valley hundreds of feet below.

Many point to some form of advanced technology, and it is a fact that most of these cities were constructed half by the Inca and half by the pre-Inca. The question up for debate is, which blocks belonged to which people? It has been further theorized that the large blocks had been moved by alien technology, or by giants, and there are compelling arguments for both theories.

It could be that the "giants" were pre-Incas, who were strong enough to move these enormously heavy blocks and that later the Inca somehow defeated them. Maybe the giants became extinct after a massive earthquake, as the area is famous for its seismic activity. There is no plausible proof yet for either theory. Another option is the "mummy in the room"—or in "Nazca," that is. Which leads us to another enigma located on the southern coast of Peru.

In early 2017, a Cusco research group found three mummies in a tomb in the Desert of Nazca. These were no ordinary mummies. They ranged in size and features. One was tall and looked like a stretched-out version of the little green men you see in Hollywood movies. She was about the size of a regular human, whereas the others were much smaller, the size of children.

All these remains featured elongated skulls and were preserved in what the expert scientists and researchers confirmed to be diatom earth. This is the same substance used to keep harmful pests under control in gardens. Also, one of these mummies was found in the fetal position looking skyward, which indicated a royal burial that ensured a proper homecoming to the afterlife—an Inca tradition.

If these mummies were from another species, then they were treated as equals by the indigenous and perhaps lived among them in their community. All the mummies had been placed in tombs, and upon further examination, the scientists noted that all the tissues and nerves were in the right places. When x-rayed, one of the mummies was found to have snakelike ribs, as well as a clutch of eggs in its stomach. So naturally, having a curious heart, I headed to track down that research group. I also hoped to see the mummies.

After scouring the internet, I found the website of an organization called the Inkari Institute, which had essentially brokered this unique discovery through a grave robber named Mario. Mario and his crew also alleged that, in addition to the other remains, they had found the body of a man with a beard—not a typical Incan trait. The combination of diatomaceous earth and dry climate preserves hair for hundreds of years.

This coincided with the rumor of Viracocha, a creator-deity legend of the local indigenous, described at times as "a white god with a beard." So, I took the next cab I could find to one of the most obscure streets in Cusco—a street that even the driver had never heard of.

When we finally arrived at our destination, the addresses weren't in order and the institute couldn't be found. Then, out of the corner of my eye I spotted a green sign that read "Vacuum Therapy." I walked to the door and stepped inside, and this very kind Danish man with an honest smile greeted me. I felt the hair on the back of my neck stand up as a sixth sense tickled my interest.

"What exactly is vacuum therapy?" I asked.

He answered, "Let me show you."

He led me into the back, past a rack of health products such as spirulina and maca (Peruvian ginseng), to an office with a couple of charts on the wall of the human body. One seemed to feature meridian lines, and another, with Spanish writing, showed pictures of teeth. We made it down the hallway and stepped into a long room full of about thirty people in reclining, wooden chair-type beds. Most of them were Incan senior citizens and probably poor. All of them had wires of some sort hooked up to them.

The doctor hitched up one of the patient's blankets, revealing that the wires were connected to large suction cups on her feet. My jaw dropped. I recognized the doctor's use of gravity to open the meridian lines—something I had learned about when I had studied Thai massage. The doctor took me into his office, and we began to rap. As it turned out, he had studied Thai massage from my own teacher's lineage in Thailand.

He explained that most diseases, as I already knew, came from an imbalance in the body. He hooked me up to his machine to relieve the neck pain that still lingered from my one and only ayahuasca experience. Three years prior I had decided to try this strong hallucinogen at an indoor ceremony in Big Sur, California. It left me at the precipice of a choice when my body reacted strongly and I couldn't exhale. My ears began to ring, and I felt something snap on the left side of my neck. I left the ceremony and went outside to lie down and die. I felt my soul leave my body. Standing at the edge of a white light, I decided that I wasn't ready to leave this life yet, and I returned.

Three years later I had a stabbing pain in the back of my neck and a burning sensation in my ear. After a two-hour session with those suction cups hooked up to my feet and hands, I felt much better, and the pain went away. We continued to talk, and I explained what I had been shown after years of meditation—about how the body has energy lines, and how those lines can be followed as if with an orthopedic scope. I imagined energy as I always did. By focusing myself as a micro-version and entering my pores into the various systems of the body and noticing blockage and/or color changes.

He showed me a chart of human teeth. "There are thirty-two teeth and each tooth represents an organ," he said. "Don't ever get a root canal."

"Why not? I'm pretty sure that I've had a few."

"As I said, each of your teeth corresponds to an organ, and when the nerve is severed then so is the energy connection. Basically, your tooth nerve sends a message to the organ, and after a root canal, the nerve believes the organ is dead. This opens a door for cancer to occur in that organ. I have seen it many times. I will have patients come in for cancer treatment. Nine times out of ten, I learn that they've had a root canal in the tooth connected to the organ."

Having already learned about the number of vertebrae in the spine at Loyola Marymount University in Los Angeles, my mind started to calculate my speculations. There are thirty-three vertebrae, each one receives a message from the brain and connects to our thirty-two teeth. I mentally counted, thirty-three vertebrae plus thirty-two teeth equals sixty-five.

In India they revere a sacred geometric mandala known as the Sri Yantra, which is made up of nine intersecting triangles. The top of the triangles faces up and the bottom triangle faces down. I discovered that there are sixty-five points in the Sri Yantra, including the very center point, which is called the Bindu. If you superimpose the Yantra over one of the Nazca Lines called the Star Glyph, it lines up perfectly.

Fig. 6 The Sri Yantra
(Image by *Hindu-Blog.com* via shutterstock.com)

Fig. 7 Star geoglyph of Nazca, Peru
(Image by Tudor Antonel Adrian via *Dreamstime Images)*

The Nazca lines consist of geometric and animal patterns out in the dry sands. Of course, there is much controversy about how and why they exist. The alien mummies I referred to earlier are from a cave-like tomb in Nazca, at an undisclosed location near the lines.

How did the ancients make use of the same sacred geometry in different locations around the world?

Now, we have another piece of evidence which indicates that the first world traveler in North America wasn't Columbus. The first beyond-reasonable-doubt scenario is that Leif Erikson, a man of Viking descent, was in the Americas around five hundred years earlier than his Spanish successor.

While there are infinite possibilities, let's explore a few conclusions. With collective consciousness we can expand or contract with theory, much like the universe does. Science that uses colonial Christianity as a lens for archeology can only take you so far. We have been limited in our consensus beliefs, which are based on who is paying for science. Much of the projects in North American archeology have been funded by Christian organizations— and especially, believe it or not, by the Mormons, who have a special, vested interest in proving a Semitic heritage migration.

Migrations to America pre-Columbus threaten the narrative of God as one person. Other religious ideas threaten an ideal. This ideal is a false history and an outdated view of society and creation.

12

MAGICO

J oseph Smith, the founder of Mormonism, was killed in the Midwest in 1844. He left a whole slew of followers who migrated to Utah, spreading the word that Smith had found evidence of an ancient migration of the Tribes of Judah. Eventually the people of Missouri labeled him a religious nut and slayed him for his sins.

These were the pilgrims' ideals, and we know now that they were not the fun-loving puritans we once had thought. They enslaved the indigenous and accused women of witchcraft, the latter a practice older than Christianity and more widespread.

It is well documented that the Mormon Church wished to prove a Semitic migration. They badly need evidence of this theory, because it would prove Joseph Smith's right to divine spiritual destiny theory. If one can get past the small sects of racist polygamists who locked up women, one might be able to see beyond the façade. Beyond entry is a smorgasbord of opportunities for resonance.

Joseph Smith was an Irishman with an interest in magic. Believing strongly in his transmissions from heaven, he practiced divination by gazing into seeing stones. One day in New York, while out in the woods during the autumnal equinox, Joe spoke with an angel named Moroni, who told him about some golden tablets buried in a mountain, which were of Jewish or Egyptian origin. They were never found.

The major problems with religion that arise for the average objective thinker is that it seems as if there is always a lost messiah, artifact, or culture awaiting verification. In this case the lost messiah was Moroni, who led Mr. Smith to the tablets. By the way, Joseph Smith's other part-time gig was that of a treasure hunter.

Smith spent most of his early twenties searching in and around his hometown of Manchester, New York. He was well known for putting his head in his hat and observing treasure through the axis of a hole in his seeing stone. Just because you make yourself well known for something doesn't mean you are an expert. In his case he just happened to be the only one around southern New York and northern Pennsylvania who bore the title of treasure hunter.

Joseph Smith simply wanted to believe that his father, who had introduced him to magic, had been the real deal. The ambition to be of worth to society has been so strong for men over the last few thousand years, it has clouded our ability to do what is right for the collective. And for Joseph Smith, the natural instinct to create something manifested no differently than for many other men in power.

Furthermore, the rejection he dealt with from mainstream

society spurred him on to prove the legitimacy of his truth. He excavated the ground of many farms, hills, and homesteads of his tiny area of the world. In other cultures, he might have been considered a shaman, because the information he pulled out of the ether was pretty remarkable. He looked into a small window in time and spied a portal to other dimensions; and if you asked him, he didn't know exactly how it worked. But in that he was no different than many other magicians who've done their thing over the past few millennia.

Joseph Smith stopped time in order to travel through it. The problem was that he had no guru, no one to expel the darkness of his illusion. If you give a man caught in his own ego an opportunity to be the authority on something, the result will be achievement-based decisions rather than something done for the greater good of the collective. We all have the ability to see the future, travel through time, and become immortal.

The treasure that Smith sought became a lie, and it compelled him into the abyss of additional lies and deceit. He was eventually thrown out of his hometown and excommunicated by his wife's family when he failed to procure a vein of silver on their homestead.

Eventually he was prosecuted for fraud and left the area for a fresh start out west. Being a big fish in a big pond might've been extremely attractive for someone who needed to prove himself and be something. So, the magician traveled west to perpetuate a cycle of destiny, and left behind holes of empty promises. Determined to have a voice, Mr. Smith decided to share his knowledge and translation of the golden tablets with Midwest America.

Along the path to religious legitimization came trials and

tribulations. The followers had to believe that there was a need for Mormonism. After purchasing a few Egyptian mummies and scrolls, he drew attention by transcribing them as further proof of an ancient Semitic migration. Joseph and his followers in Ohio were persecuted for their beliefs. An angry mob beat the piss out of them and tarred and feathered them.

Joseph claimed to know shorthand Egyptian writing—a simplified version designed to make Egyptian writing easier to translate. The people of the great state of Ohio wouldn't stand for his blasphemous interpretations of the word of God. The Mormons headed farther west to Missouri, amassing even more of a following. Eventually, facing more persecution, Joe took the stance of a cornered rat and bit back.

He staged rallies for the Mormons' right to be free from persecution. With ideas already too big for America, they took their cause to the streets of Nauvoo, Illinois. Presenting ideas of polygamy and backing it all with a five-thousand-person militia, Joseph decided to run for president. Before that would ever become a reality, his organization lost further credibility. He was brought in for charges of perjury and polygamy.

By the time Mr. Smith and his brother Hyrum turned themselves in, the hate-fueled charges had become more severe. Malignant preaching simply could not be tolerated, especially when it translated into sexual freedom. The locals locked them up in the jailhouse, where they awaited trial.

But, of course, any good story of a cancerous revolutionary ends with an angry mob marching toward the courthouse. On June 27, 1844, the inevitable happened: the townspeople rose up in mob form and broke down the doors to the jail, shooting Hyrum in the face. Joseph Smith put up an irrelevant fight for a few moments, before hurling himself face first to the dusty streets below.

There is no doubt in my mind that Smith possessed a special gift, and that all of us have latent within us. He was a shamanic diviner, a Master of Water; but he, like so many other men with war in their hearts, succumbed to the power of dark consciousness.

All in all, his ideas might have been more accepted if he had stayed within the framework of society, but he chose instead to use his illusions to fuel mastery. He was, like so many leaders, a Kundalini master and a magician.

I learned that the Book of Mormon speaks of the tribe of Lehi, which traveled to North America and settled in a narrow neck of land on the edge of the plentiful. According to Mormon scholars, that place was the Isthmus of Tehuantepec, located in southern Mexico. I investigated the possibility.

My first stop was Veracruz, situated at the northern point of the isthmus. I arrived at the airport late, with not only a hunger for knowledge, but for tacos. Nothing was open near the hotel. I cased the area, and quickly realized that the cheaply priced "good looking" hotel I'd booked online had been planted in a dicey neighborhood.

I walked at a brisk pace with my eyes forward, toward the light—when I noticed that I was being followed by an aggressive group of seven transvestite hookers. One, who sported an eleven-o'clock shadow, pulled down her shirt with a loud whistle, and said, "Come over here and fuck me." I tried to act natural, and asked,

"*¿Donde esta comida?*" ("Where can I buy some food?")

They pointed down the street, but I quickly realized that the only thing down the street was a dark alley full of makeshift bedrooms for prospective clients. I thought, what shameless promotion. Don't transvestite hookers live by a code? I suppose I give people too much credit.

13

BON VOYAGE

The next morning, I took a cab to see what used to be known as the first pre-Mayan example of the isthmus-style hieroglyphs. Although the Mayan civilization existed around the time that stela was carved, it's considered Olmec in origin and dates to 32 BC. That was right around the time when the Tree of Life stela was carved in Itzapa, on the west side of the isthmus. It depicted two teachers traveling in a boat.

In the mid-1900s, a Norwegian by the name of Thor Heyerdahl traveled from Peru to French Polynesia in "just" one hundred days. He sailed in what was basically a pontoon boat made of Balsa wood that he and his crew had cut from timber not far from the Amazon jungle. Heyerdahl proved that one doesn't need a large or advanced vessel to travel the high seas. I am convinced that all anyone would need to make the journey is knowledge of the trade winds, a good boat, and cooperative weather.

It is written in religious texts how miracles and magic were used by Christ, Buddha, Padmasambhāva. When a group of indigenous people, who were earth-based in religion and lifestyle, saw the feats performed by these travelers, they couldn't help but associate them with the gods whom they perceived to rule nature, and the sun, moon, and stars.

When you're a child on a playground, the peer you look to as a leader is usually someone who appears more intelligent, stronger and especially charismatic. It is not a stretch of the imagination to consider that, if you are blessed with all of these qualities, and possess esoteric knowledge, especially in ancient times, you'll wield extreme clout. Throw in a few symbols that appear in an indigenous people's cosmology, and—voilà!—a god is born.

The Maya put their trust in magicians to run the show. Eventually, when the climate changed, the sorcerers fell short of their promise of successful agriculture. Their entire existence can be extrapolated into bio-indications for change in present day society.

When I was twenty-two, a friend died. He was burnt up in a car after passing out from a long night of drinking. I had recently read a little of the Tibetan Book of the Dead. After my friend's wake, we had a party to celebrate his life. The book is basically a set of instructions for a safe passage into the afterlife, and none other than Timothy Leary introduced it to the American public in 1964.

I was inspired to share some local psychoactive mushrooms I had picked a few days prior as a means for us to help pass our friend's soul into the underworld. I made tea on a stove, using about an ounce of the mushrooms. I cooked them down into a black sludge and shared the product I'd created with a couple of friends.

I immediately noticed the results, and the kitchen walls began to breathe as if they possessed a pair of lungs. I pretended that this wouldn't be a ride to remember and went outside to process the gravity of my choice.

There I was, sitting outside with my head in my hands, saddened by my friend's death—mostly because his wife and newborn child were now without a husband and a father—not to mention that his brother was one of the participants. When I removed my head from my hands and looked up in tears, I observed a strange phenomenon. I couldn't believe my eyes. The front lawn had turned into the front page of a newspaper. Only I could tell it wasn't the current local paper. It appeared to be from the early 1900s, as one of the photos featured an old-style car with skinny, white-walled tires.

My head fell back into my hands. When I resurfaced from an abyss of colors, I saw an altogether different headline. This one was of what appeared to be ancient origin, written in stone. I was completely certain that I had never seen it before.

About ten years later I was in Singapore learning to meditate, and the memory of that mushroom-induced vision came rushing into my consciousness. I asked myself, "What is this about?" Then I was transported to another memory. Only this recollection was not from my current life. I had a beard, long red hair, and in my hands, I could feel cold, wet prison bars. Into my head popped a name, a year, and the phrase "Red River Scandinavian." When I looked it up on the Internet the next day, I was directed to the Kensington Rune stone.

This notorious piece of stone, discovered in Minnesota in 1898, bears early Germanic or Scandinavian rune-style writing, and reads, "Eight Goths and twenty-two Norwegians on an exploration journey from Vinland to the west. We had camp by two skerries [small ships] one-day's journey from this stone. We were [out] to fish one day. After we came home [we] found ten men red with blood and tortured. Hail Virgin Mary. Save [us] from evil. [We] have ten men by the sea to look after our ships, fourteen days' journey from this island. [In the] year 1362."

If I were to extrapolate from this experience, I would say that time is cyclical and we are offered chances, at times, to awaken to the possibility of engaging in a life more authentic to the calling of our soul. It is up to us whether we take notice of these singular events or continue to sleep. Now, granted, a lot of us have been asleep for many years, but this is nothing compared to the actual potential of how old this world and our souls are.

These experiences and reflections helped me to piece together the forgotten history of humanity.

Most people ignore the signs on the floor of the desert of Nazca, and the connection with earlier inhabitants. I am talking about Pre-Inca, since the actual Incan time period was only two hundred years. We are led to believe that our species as an advanced society has existed for ten thousand years or less, yet the proof otherwise is staggering.

This leaves us grasping for a connection to the old paradigm where women are inferior to men because of physicality or being less logical. This in-the-box thinking has prompted us to leave all the real mysteries to left-brain thinkers. However, the time period of enigmas like this one was synonymous with mysticism and portals to other worlds of perception.

It was in Nazca that the psychoactive San Pedro cactus had an influence on a culture, which was rooted in connections with the sun, moon, and stars. You will also see a lateral conjunction to the equinoxes and solstices, like the Maya. The shaman was the go-to administrator between worlds, on the wings of the Serpent and the God of Air. This is all clearly depicted on their brightly colored pottery.

Could it be possible that the Nazca people were tapping into the same dimension as other ancients from around the world? Or was it that the ancients weren't from this world? Either way, I knew something out of this world was buried in the desert.

14

PARACAS

P aracas, Peru, is located south of Lima about three hours by car. Paracas means "the place of wind and sand." It has a very dry climate and is part of the Atacama Desert, which extends further south into Chile, making for perfect conditions for the preservation of bodies, skeletons, and textiles. It is also known for its fishing and tourism.

Located just at the southern entrance to the town, on the left side of the street, is the Julio C. Tello Museum, which houses a few unusual curiosities: the ancient elongated skulls. Julio, now deceased, was a local man who found the museum's skulls in a graveyard, along with a few hundred other remains.

The skulls are about thirty percent larger by volume than most human skulls. They have only one suture connection on the top, as well as some interestingly unique nerve pathways just above where the top vertebrae connects. Also, the eye sockets are much larger, and the skull thicker, than that of the average human. Since the Paracas Desert has virtually no rainfall, the mummies still retain much of their blond and red hair. Tests have been done, funded by the world's leading authority on these types of skulls. The tests revealed that the DNA of these skulls is not human as we know it.

Digging deeper we find that more expensive tests must be done to obtain more conclusive results. Apparently, those tests would cost upward of one hundred thousand dollars. The skulls, however, can be traced back to Northeastern European descent, somewhere close to the Black Sea. Here is a connection in time, space, and history. It is my belief that visitation and colonization from ancient mariners occurred on the diversely rich shores of Paracas.

These visits happened numerous times over the course of many thousands of years. For the same reason that the Maya knew the Spanish would show up, and knew of the cross, maybe the people of Paracas and Nazca were aware beforehand of a coming migration of hypothetical gods or a race of teachers. When groups of people are tapped into a frequency based on the cycles of the earth, sun, and moon, time as a linear element can be transcended.

One of the men initially involved in testing the elongated skulls of Paracas was L.A. Marzulli. He has entertained a theory based on the biblical verses of Genesis 6:4: "There were giants in the earth in those days; and also after that, when the sons of God came in unto the daughters of men, and they bear children to them, the same became mighty men which were of old, men of renown." Marzulli states that these skulls are from the offspring of the fallen angels called Nephilim, who mated with the human women on Mount Caucasus, northeast of Turkey. He also claims they were nearly all killed, but the few who survived found their way to Paracas. Could they have been the fallen angels or extra-terrestrials or ancient mariners?

Brien Foerster, a biologist who made the skulls famous, has teamed up with Marzulli. They hope to probe this further, and drill deeper into the skulls of the Paracas. Only time will tell.

Another thread woven into the Paracas textiles themselves is the striking similarities to the art and characters of the Turkish rugs. In the east and other places, we see stunning art in what's called hooks, the act of threading symbols into the rug with a hook. With all hooks reflecting another time when the Paracas were not Paracas—they were Turkish and, ultimately, red-haired people with Rh Negative blood and larger skulls.

One of the enigmatic wonders of Paracas is something the local tour guides call the "Candelabra." Situated on an island just off the coast is a giant drawing in the sand, etched into the side of a hill. It appears like the Nazca lines, as you can see it from the air and sea, and it measures about six hundred feet tall. It features three columns, with the center being the tallest and at the top. Stems sprout out from the sides as if they were branches.

Many have said that "Candelabra" is a drawing of the hallucinogenic cactus, San Pedro, while others speculate that it is a monument to the God Viracocha, representing thunder. The etching has definitely been used for navigation, helping to guide ships into the port of Paracas, but was it used in the same manner in ancient times?

I arrived in Paracas in late 2017, still reflecting on a previous visit in 2010, on the same occasion when my ex-wife and I sped in a taxicab away from the oncoming tsunami, and all the locals stood on the roofs of the restaurants and waited for the flood. At the time I had no plans to return. Neither would I have guessed then that that brief visit to this place would produce such a reflection from memory lane.

The next morning the breakfast buffet hall was filled to the brim with large, retired Hollanders. They were shoveling five types of meat into their mouths while clogging the toaster line. They ignored me, which suited me just fine. Being a "ghost" in this resort hotel was just what the mystic hermit ordered. As I jumped on a boat to go see this "tree thing," I noticed a mass of Dutch folks jammed into it. I grabbed a bright orange life jacket and decided philosophically to merge with the inevitable.

My new family and I made it to the island where the tree was located, and we stopped for a visit. The tour guide, sporting one of those white yacht hats with a yellow cord, spoke in Dutch and Spanish before letting me in on the scoop.

"For over fifty years people have harvested the phosphorus-rich seabird guano of the Ballestas Islands and sold it to Americans for farming fertilizer," explains the tour guide.

The closer I got to the source of all that fertilizer, the more I wanted to turn around. There must have been a million birds dive-bombing the plankton in the sea. My nose was burning with the powerful ammonia smell beyond comfort, beyond reason, but these Dutch folks had paid good money for the tour. I knew better than to rock the boat; I would have lost. Plus, I wanted to see the cute little penguins that also made those islands their home. Apparently, the guano collectors who lived on the islands used to eat them, and as a result the local penguin population became endangered.

We passed through a stone archway covered in sunbathing sea lions. The guide began to speak of the rich biological diversity, and how the cycle of life played such an important role here.

The Candelabra is also called the "Trident" or the "Cactus" or the "Candelabra of the Andes."

Just a few days prior to this I was north of the desert in the capital of Lima, at the Larco Museum, which consisted of two floors crammed full of pottery from Nazca. While gazing at the distinctive artwork—depictions of the region's land, sea, and sky— I noticed something. Not only was the art crafted with symmetrically accurate zoomorphic animal bodies, but some of the pots also depicted human faces.

On some of them were what appeared to be cross-sections of the San Pedro cactus. It takes many years for San Pedro to grow until it is ready to be picked and made into a tea. Where the ayahuasca is said to be the feminine, San Pedro is masculine. That is to say, the two natural hallucinogens each work on the respective quality within the individual.

This could lend to the idea that the people of Paracas used San Pedro for the center of their society, and that many other people from other cultures around the globe consider this area to be a spiritual Mecca. Due to the influence of a culture from the other side of the globe, it is most likely that this geoglyph was used as a sort of daytime lighthouse for ancient mariners.

I don't believe in accidents. I never really have unless I was passing the salt and spilled a drink. Everything usually happens for a reason, at least to someone somewhere. Maybe the salt gets spilled, and a Japanese company makes billions.

The boat dropped us off at the harbor, and I returned to my hotel and took a nap while waiting for the next tour.

15

EVOLUTION

I jumped into a van with a local man named Juan, who had helped me book the previous tour. We left town and followed a trail of glitter-like sand that littered the highway and seemed to have fallen out of the back of semi-trucks. The driver explained that there was a Japanese salt mining operation in the preserve, and the trucks were hauling the salt to the harbor to be shipped to the United States and Canada. But that wasn't the only thing that has been shipped out of the reserve.

"Nearly thirty million years of rich evolutionary history has left many mineral deposits in that desert," he told me. "Up until recently, there used to be oil, copper, iron, gold, mica, and quartzite mining. But the Peruvian government decided to shut down all operations in the reserve due to excess pollution in the region. They were all foreign investors, anyway."

Juan then showed me the mica buried in the sand. I picked up a piece and followed the vein in the sand, and I noticed there was a boatload of this stuff. It occurred to me that mica had many uses in electrical applications.

We pulled off to the side of the road in the middle of nowhere to begin the tour. The sun was hot, and the wind burned my face, stinging my eyes. This dry climate was cool yet unforgiving. Squinting, I sat in awe of where I was: one of the driest places on the planet, yet it possessed a vibrancy that couldn't be ignored.

As we followed a short path with lined-up rocks marking the trail, Juan showed me the fossilized remains of an ancient invertebrate called *turritella woodsi*. Looking at this ice cream cone-shaped snail from which many species had evolved, I thought that every once in a while, a species comes into the mix and shakes the tree or demands that it evolve and creates punctuated equilibrium.

That most definitely happened in Paracas.

We drove to where the sand met the ocean, viewing a massive cathedral of stone—the actual location where the conclusion of the original Planet of the Apes film had been filmed. I reflected further that, if there had been alien visitors, there is a chance they might have needed these superconductors to power their ship, and the DNA of the fossils to conduct experiments with, or to keep certain crossbreeds in production.

Does our intelligence grant us a warrant to feel superior? What if our creator wasn't God, as we know Him? Would it be such a blow to the human ego to accept the possibility that our species had been domesticated for the purposes of a biological experiment?

We have bred livestock for food, for their hides, and even for fertilizer. We've genetically modified hybridized plants and farmed fish. All the backbreaking work has been done by the lowest common denominator in the food chain: the poor. Our food, fertilizer, and resources are grown, harvested and extracted.

Everyone wants a job to feed their family, to make a living, and to have a better life like they see Americans enjoying. This paradigm perpetuates the colonialist lifestyle. Years pass and not much changes, because it is the colonialists who want to sell Coca Cola, Starbucks, and American football as status. All the while, this cultural behemoth is drastically changing life on earth as we know it. We are literally sucking the earth dry of its minerals.

The Paracas Reserve itself is a perfect example of the Tree of Life. Not only is the Tree literally written in the sand, but the plants, minerals, and animals all work together in an organized chaos in order to weed out the weakest of the various species.

Some people live their lives never thinking that there could be other dimensions, other worlds, other civilizations and relatives of our species. I'm talking about the interconnectedness of it all and the acknowledgment of our ancestors but not just the human ones. How they have all played a part in this grand symphony, playing the instruments of an intimate orchestral web of life.

We sit back in luxury while our planet is dying. The infinite riches that we enjoy are an essential ingredient in a recipe buried in the desert and frozen in the tundra. If there is a creator, then life can be created again. But if that creator is in the form of intelligent life on some other planet or in another dimension, then maybe we have gotten more chances than they care to give us. Either way, right now we are blowing our chance. But there is hope.

Every time you hear about the injustice of a woman who's

been sexually assaulted, a black man shot by the police, or even a child abused by a Hollywood actor, maybe we should consider that it is through the darkness now being illuminated that we can ultimately correct ourselves and evolve and thrive as a species. That pinpoint of light is where consciousness originates.

If the old paradigm is failing and slowly dying, like the earth and its inhabitants, then what can we do as a species to survive? It is almost as if it's a race; and it is. We are the ones who called it the "human race." Competition is all we have known, because we have used the patriarchal method for virtually everything. It has been used for expansion and for agriculture, but also out of fear of not having enough. We have trashed the earth because we feared our own sexuality, as well as that of others.

Women are a precious gift, not a possession. Countless numbers of them have been raped and deemed as property. How many have been burned because of their knowledge and power that came from a connection to Mother Earth? This skewed view of women is a sickness, but like any other sickness there is usually a cause and a cure. The cure sure as hell isn't reverse shaming or more violence, and it isn't holding back affection or unconditional love. It is education.

America and the world are now warming up to the idea that maybe jail, punishment, and shame isn't a successful venture in the long run. The "war on drugs" not only cost us millions, but also resulted in our nonviolent brothers, fathers, sisters, mothers, and children being incarcerated. Some of these prison sentences are many years just for smoking a doobie. As the western political system exacerbates itself toward extinction, we're seeing a shift in perspective.

There is no school for ethical treatment of the "other." Many men and women see others as competition, and rightfully so. Our DNA has been influenced in such a way that if we turn our backs for a moment, some other schmuck will fish in our pond. The fact is, it isn't our pond and never was. The choice of love lies in the essence of expressing true timelessness in every moment.

How can we as humans stand up and stop the ongoing warfare that has been a staple since the emergence of agriculture and religion?

After reflecting on all of this, I snapped back to the present. Juan turned to me and commented, "Maybe we're the aliens, huh?"

16

THE EQUINOX

After returning from Peru, something puzzled me. As I sat in meditation an image came to me of the seeds of the white flower in Belize that Maria had offered me a year prior. This opened an inquiry into this white flower she dubbed "Lol-K'in", which, as I've mentioned before, means "flower of the sun" in Mayan.

Maria originally moved to Belize from the Yucatan with her sisters when she was a young adult. It was from the very region where she was born that the text of the book of "Chilam Balaam" originated. Chilam Balaam means "jaguar prophet". The work was rumored to have been originally translated through a man who lived in the fifteenth century. This old text, a hybrid of Mayan cosmology and Catholicism, was pieced together in the eighteenth and nineteenth centuries.

Friar and Bishop Diego de Landa burned much of the ancient Mayan written tradition, which left mostly an oral history largely influenced by Christian colonialism. The original cosmological vision was illustrated in the Chilam Balaam, but with a few exceptions. In it we see a history of how the Spanish conquered each city. This book even contains the military movements and conquests by the Late Classic rulers of the Itza and is not limited to customs through ritual sacrifice and herbal medicine.

These rituals are described as often including a flower. The Mexican anthropologist Ralph L. Roys theorized that this flower was *Plumeria rubra*—a tropical flower that grows around the world, especially in Hawaii. But the true origins of the flower are actually in Central America. This fact might indicate that the trade routes weren't limited to the last five hundred years, as previously thought. Understanding the migration of certain plant species would certainly help humanity understand the genesis of our own species.

Was the Lol-K'in the same as the Plumeria, or was it something more psychoactive in nature? By tracing the roots of the ethnogeny practice, we can discern the branches of the Maya. If trading was done, then it is reasonable to say that wherever the people traveled so did their chemistry set. The *Rivea Corymbosa*—or Ololiuqui, as the Aztecs called it—contains ergot, the same fungus that attacks grain. It is similar to LSD, although it is called LSA.

In the book of Chilam Balaam there is also an account of the Itza and their exodus to Petén, Guatemala. It was through the white flower that they were brought to the south. In this case the "white flower" was a princess named Sak Nikte (Mayan for "white flower"). An arranged marriage was promised to the ruler Hunac Ceel, but a warrior and true love kidnapped her instead. They fled to modern day Belize and Guatemala, and the city was lost to the people of the Itz. The Itz symbolized the dewdrop of creation. It was described as anything that drops in liquid form, especially semen and menstrual blood. The first morning dew was synonymized here, as well.

The Maya believed in the creation of opposing forces, as well as the great cycles of time. Where did they get these ideas? Were they just something that occurred to them from living in sync with natural rhythms? Or did they originate with visitors from another culture?

In early 2018, I visited Tulum once more, and I noticed how things had changed. One too many yogis had posted pictures of themselves posing in front of crystal blue cenotes (natural sinkhole pools). This caused a lemming-like effect of mildly inspiring quotes and endless hashtag streams as numerous as the sinkholes in the Yucatan. Descent is a common theme in Tulum, where you see the god of bees and war as an embodiment of Venus and Kukulkán. This serpent energy represents both destruction and creation. In the classic Hindu text, the Vedas, Shiva wore a snake around his neck.

Joseph Campbell spoke of certain figures, symbols, or animals perennially guiding humans for personal growth and transformation. These subconscious symbols have been at work since the dawn of time. We stand now at an important juncture regarding the war in our hearts. Let us remember the lessons of a forgotten past. We are missing a vitally important component of compassion.

Why did men burn women? Why was the tradition of the goddess suppressed? The simple answer is that their motivation was fear.

As early as the first century BC, an assault on the earth in Central America began. The Snake Dynasty paved the jungle with limestone, extracted every mineral possible, used all of the water sources, and enslaved those who could be subjugated. This was done in the name of a serpent, which in the goddess tradition represented the great cycles of the earth. Then again, we see a return of symbolism with the name Isis being used in the Middle East by a group of racist and sexist murderers. By using the Egyptian goddess's name to represent their terrorist agenda, they have tarnished it forever.

Across the globe from Central America, in southeastern Turkey, is a place called Mount Nemrut. There, an interesting parallel can be drawn. This was the only other place where time was worshiped as in Central America. We also see their evidence of the worship of the cat, bird, and snake: hallmarks of the Central and South American indigenous peoples.

Right in front of the mountain are ancient ruins dating from around the first century BC. Lined up in a row are kings with long beards and pointy hats, and a woman wearing a hat that appears to be Greek.

In the Popol Vuh, the creation story found in Chichicastenango, Guatemala, the Maya wrote of their ancestors coming from a "place of dawn to the east." On Stela Five in Izapa is a Tree of Life carving, depicting a man and possibly a woman in a boat. The man has a pointy hat and wears a beard, while the woman has on a hat like one seen on a statue at Mount Nemrut. Both are teaching the youth. It's possible that around the first or second century BC, these two got in a boat, sailed from the Mediterranean across the Atlantic, and landed in what is now current day Veracruz, Mexico. This historic event could have taken place between the eras of the

Huasteca and the Olmecs—before the Mayan civilization.

It is possible that when these Turks sailed west, they spread the ancient knowledge of Zoroastrianism. They were well received not only because of their parallel animism theories, but due to their worship of fire and time as well. On the left side of Stela Five, you can see the exact same fire symbol as that of Zoroastrianism.

On the Caribbean side of Mexico, the Post-Classic ruins of Tulum are situated right above the ocean. The site was used for trade. Most of the stelae have some type of picture of Chaac or Ixchel connected to the energy of water. I believe that Tulum was more than just a seaport trading post; I view it as once a Mecca of ancient feminine wisdom.

My last visit was in 2012. Back then it was not a family vacation destination, and it sure as hell wasn't a place for parading women dripping in stone jewelry and flowing robes—at least, not in the fashion of the hashtag epidemic. This time I was there because I wanted to show Mexico to my girlfriend, and I figured this would be a safe bet, the alternative being a campaign through the jungle in search of a random snake king, which would have been a waste of our time. Half a year later, National Geographic released a special on LIDAR and the serpent kings.

LIDAR is an acronym for Light Detection and Ranging. It works by flying a plane above the jungle and shooting, through foliage, photon light lasers which detect topography. The archeologist in the program took a computer tablet out to the Petén region and peered into the jungle. The group uncovered a pyramid, as well as the remains of an entire settlement that encompassed as many as a million or more inhabitants.

Technology is funny, because it outclasses the archeologist who actually toiled away in the jungle to achieve his findings. Now you just need to be tech savvy and inspired. I pictured the original gringo, who "found" this area, being shocked when he learned of the new discovery. Or maybe he was gratified that someone furthered the research that he had started so many years ago.

The gringo director of El Mirador, Dr. Richard Hansen, seemed to be excited about the find. I think it will probably herald more funding for his research. He no doubt realized that uncovering the whole civilization was going to take tens of millions of dollars and more time than he has left in this life. So perhaps National Geographic and the Fox Network have the kind of bucks that will get to the bottom of the pile of codices burned by Friar Diego de Landa in the mid-fifteenth century in Mani, Yucatan.

Underneath all this architecture, art, and history is the classic example of the Mayan Tree of Life. In most of the sites a symbolic version of the story was built into their architecture. Kukulkán, who is represented as serpent through animism, was God, much like the Holy Spirit of Christ as man or as an interchangeable energy in the roots of Christianity, Judaism paralleling Kundalini of the Vedic tradition.

Kukulkán acted as the guide of people's souls into the underworld after death. The idea of this transition was designed into the arrangement of the city of Chichen Itza. Picture a visual yet metaphorical procession from the pyramid through an underground passageway below the white road, which leads to the Gran Cenote—the gateway to the underworld.

The Gran Cenote is hundreds of feet deep. In the rainy

season, it is clear blue in color. It has been dredged over the years since the early nineteenth century. The dredging has yielded many finds, such as golden knives, jade necklaces, but more importantly, bones. These bones were the remains of hundreds of men, women and children from all around Central America. The high priests of Chichen Itza, the stewards of that process, conducted the sacrifices.

You can see on all the brilliant stucco buildings a regurgitation of the Temple Teotihuacan in Mexico City. It is very evident that this work was more Aztec than Maya. Most everything is covered in white skull bricks, eagle carvings, and large, bright, white snakes—the same as Teotihuacan.

The snake kings, or Cannul, were running most of the show from what is now current day Mexico City. They had the advantages of superior size, weaponry, and trading capabilities. They were master manipulators. So, they showed up with massive promises of protection, unity, and commerce for the current rulers. More importantly, they brought promises of a long prosperous rulership and peace. Does this sound familiar?

When some of the less important rulers refused, the snake kings cleverly turned the minor allies against each other, thus initiating more and more conflict. This same dynamic takes place today, just as it has since the beginning.

The day before, I walked the sacbes (paved Mayan white roads) of Coba. It boasts the most sacbes in the region, if not in all of the land of the Maya. More noncoincidental coincidences revealed that a great female leader had ruled this area.

Further down the Mayan rabbit hole, walking down sacbe number nine, I noticed there was a stela halfway to the site. Was this sacbe deliberately placed here for a procession of death, metaphorical or otherwise? One of the white roads in this site continues for nearly a hundred kilometers west to Yaxuna, a Pre-Classic gem "discovered" by Sylvanus Morley in the early nineteenth century. Later that day I decided to go see it.

The blue sky above was in the traditional Yucatan style, full of fluffy white clouds moving at high velocity across the sun. As soon as I began to take that in, I noticed a sign pointing to an immediate left, toward what appeared to be an unexcavated pyramid. I turned the wheel hard as I carefully navigated the rental car down a bumpy road. A man popped up out of nowhere with an INAH (Mexico's National Institute of Anthropology and History) shirt, wearing a scowl and carrying a deer rifle as he strode toward me. I arrived at the site to see another local man lying in a hammock under a palapa, or grass hut.

I signed my name on his sheet, and he offered his services as a guide for two hundred pesos. It was hotter than the nine levels of Xibalba as I began to hike to the top of a small pyramid that overlooked the white road, which headed east all the way back to Coba. Just behind us was a larger pyramid that he explained was submerged in seventy meters of dirt and rubble.

My guide told a story of psychedelic honey enemas that induced trance and ritual dancing—where women would dress in brightly colored bird feather outfits, and the men would perform a shamanic ritual honoring Wakan Chan, the World Tree. The liquid used in their enemas was balché, a strong beer made from fermented honey. He explained that this balché was most likely mixed with Lol-K'in, the flower of the sun!

Yaxuna was constructed in the same fashion as many Pre-Classic sites to the south, using a triad of pyramids to venerate the gods of the sky, the earth, and a "watery place." This triad is said to reflect the three stars in the belt of the Orion constellation. The gods are brothers dubbed G1, G2, and G3, born not too far apart in relative time and space.

In the center of the triangular constellation of the Orion Nebula is M42, the cosmic hearthstone, and the very fire of creation that creates stars. How did the Maya know this? Archeologists point to what the Maya call "the Vision Serpent." They find in it the soul's journey to the afterlife, with death and creation synonymous as one.

17

THE WEAVING

T he word yoga means "to yoke or join." The yoga of physical postures that many people are familiar with is called asana, which means "the seat." It is within the teachings of Hatha, which means "sun and moon." So Hatha Yoga would be, by definition, to yoke the sun and the moon.

The sun stands for the masculine and the moon, the feminine. Each represents a side of the body from which the energy rises like a serpent interlocking at energy centers along the spine called chakras. Taking a closer look, we see striking similarities to the cosmology of the Palenque Maya and yoga of large proportion.

It is almost as if the world's cosmology were interconnected or presented by one source. Many have asked the questions related to this of "how, why, and when."

Modern day archeologists fall short of the truth based on society and religion. UFO enthusiasts do most of the extensive research in this field of study, and ancient alien theorists on Discovery Channel almost always answer "yes" to the weighty question of whether all unexplained archeology is alien in nature.

A leading authority on ancient civilizations, Graham Hancock, points instead to early sea mariners. I believe this to be a wonderful alternative to speculative works pioneered by Erich von Däniken, where the norm is usually a spaceship using outdated industrial technology. The deeper teachings of yoga are a universal expression quite literally written in stone on the temples and shrines spanning continents worldwide. The same symbols that manifest energy have been long forgotten. Hancock speaks of precise degrees during the precession of the equinoxes and solstices, many of which I have witnessed.

If the Catholic cross, Mayan cross, Inca cross, Knights Templar and Kabbalah were superimposed on the image of the Sri Yantra, the angles would line up seamlessly. We see that all religions, no matter their geographic origins, used the same symbol to attempt to solve the very human problem of death.

Cosmic hearthstone cosmology is nothing new under the sun and was born in one of the sunniest places on earth: Egypt. The classic example of this concept is the placement of the three pyramids of Giza, as they line up perfectly with the Orion constellation belt, as well. The members of the Egyptian ruling class, like the Maya, were obsessed with death, trying to prove to the common people the legitimacy of their rule by showing their connections to the gods. At death they would return to the source, the fire of creation in the center of the cosmos. In this instance, however, the supreme mother and father were Osiris and Isis, rather than the Hero Twins of the Popol Vuh.

When I think objectively, I consider it possible that humanity is extraterrestrial, only I wouldn't conclude that the gods were so. If the ancients could glean a reason for the weather patterns, and explain the purposes of the sun, moon, and stars, then they could've felt comfortable with their projected immortality. A chance for redemption of the soul, offered by one or many explainable infinite sources, could be possible. It's not that any single belief system or civilization has brought us closer to understanding: they all have.

And that includes the teachings of the Jewish, Zoroastrian, Catholic, Chinese, Egyptian, Roman, Polynesian, Viking, and African peoples. This grouping pretty much covers most continents and religions, apart from the Aborigines of Australia.

The Maya had a unique number system called the "long count." It was a method for writing a huge sum of years in a small space on their stelae. They depicted and recorded events such as a ruler coming to power, a war that happened, or even a celestial event.

One of the first recorded uses was in the state of Veracruz near the Gulf Coast in 36 BC at a place called Tres Zapotes in Olmec country.

The twelve tribes of Israel, when united in the "New Jerusalem", were to number 144,000. The Mormons believe these people were to be priests. While a baktun, a Mayan measurement, numbers 144,000 days. Maybe it is all just a giant game of ancient telephone, where we see a continual migration of seafaring groups from faraway lands influencing the Maya.

I believe in magic. Not like Penn and Teller nowadays, sporting hair dye and pulling elaborate rabbits from their asses.

This was (and is) the real deal. A renaissance of time in civilization as we know it. It could be that there is a recipe for this magic that has long been forgotten and that we are waking up to now. A potent combination of collective consciousness that is a ripe exploration, just like the fruit of the Garden of Eden, and the Maya were destined to reveal this. It is no secret that many leaders had control over large populations through their great charisma or energy. These people were using the magic I'm referring to. This magic was and is Kundalini, the energy of the serpent.

The deity Kukulkán could have been an extraterrestrial serpent, but the only evidence for this is hypothetical. We can go there if you are interested. First, consider this: if most religions have a record in stone of the serpent as a supernatural force, then I am led to believe that is no coincidence.

The serpent symbolized the route of energy in the spine. This energy is timeless, since it is the same as the cerebral spinal fluid that facilitates serotonin spikes with DMT in the pineal gland. These same spikes can be achieved through ayahuasca, meditation, dancing and, especially, sex. It is euphoria that brings us to a non-dual state of the mind, and into the tiny place of Christ (aka Kukulkán).

While in that state, the consciousness of the heart destroys the illusion of separation of the mind. It is that illusion that drew humanity into this mess in the first place, and it is the very thing that will get us out. That is why the Maya believed in the underworld and celebrated duality as a necessity . . . which eventually leads to non-duality. It is illustrated in their cosmological artwork time and again.

That moment of merging with non-duality has been taught to the masses through Buddhism, and there are those who have tapped into that state of consciousness, procuring precognitive results. Edgar Cayce, who was a Christian, is a great example. Living in the early 1900s, he was one of the first psychic mediums in recorded history. Nicknamed the "sleeping prophet," he did just that. By entering a somnolent, trancelike state, he tapped into Akasha, or the Akashic records.

While helping many thousands with their issues of health and wealth, Cayce predicted many outcomes that came true. Here lies yet another parallel to the Mayan Cosmo vision and those of others from around the globe. Speaking of such things, I digress to Palenque where hundreds of academic scholars, archeologists, and New Age folks have speculated on K'inich Janaab' Pakal the Great's origin, based on the magnificent artwork carved into the lid of his sarcophagus.

Fig. 8 Pakal the Great's Sarcophagus Lid
(Image courtesy of *Matthew Pallamary*)

The misinformation started when Erich von Däniken wrote
Chariot of the Gods in the late 1960s, describing Pakal as an

astronaut. Decades later the History Channel chose to run the television series, Ancient Aliens. The show's host and guests elaborated conclusions based on von Däniken's ideas, where instead of the Tree of Life lineage concept, a Hollywood set maker added mechanical objects to the artwork, and even drew Pakal using a breathing apparatus. He had a great imagination, but he also played on the imagination of the show's host, who already believed that everything unexplained in ancient culture was extraterrestrial.

The art of Palenque was like no other, thanks to Pakal and his offspring. We see what appears to be an Asian influence of not only elaborate stucco glyphs and stelae, but also stories of ancient visionary historical downloads. The tale of cosmic legitimacy for rule literally permeated the walls of the most uniquely enigmatic city in all of Mesoamerica, and perhaps the world. Not only do the glyphs tell a story, but they also furnish a legacy upstaging any potential successor . . . except for Pakal's son, of course.

Who would argue that you couldn't possibly have a connection with the gods of creation, if it is all magnificently depicted in a timeless way that can confuse your average corn grower, stone mover, or tree chopper? No other city told the creation story like Palenque did—a story of three gods, representing where stars are born and die. The ceiba tree stands in the place of the World Tree, representing the upper, middle, and underworlds. The Tomb of Pakal the First shouts "as above, so below" loud and clear.

Maybe he was an ancient astronaut; but, just as an advanced yogi can astral travel to the time and space continuums of other planets, so could a Mayan ruler. And travel he did, especially under the influence of the psychedelic mushrooms that grow wild in the marshlands right outside the city. Sprinkle in a bit of precise synchronistic timing based on mathematics and cosmic alignments, and voilà!

This was the original time machine, and not a junior science fair rocket ship propelled by fuel. It was propelled by the third eye with high serotonin spikes in the central nervous system that produced DMT. This, in my experience, is the way to not only create cosmic synchronicity, but to experience precognition.

In Palenque the rulers were not only immortalized through the magic of the Sri Yantra, but Kundalini-like electricity rose from the water embodying the serpent connecting with the sky, creating true immortality. This reality was literally cemented in the city's real name of Lakhamna, which means "big water," as in "the eternal." Pakal was a magician. Not unlike many other rulers, he showed the people his power—but something was different here. While waging war, he also created art.

If anyone was an incarnation of ancient rulers, I think Pakal was, symbolically or otherwise. Revolutionary New Age artist and Mayanist José Argüelles called him "Pakal Votan." Votan, a legendary Mayan time traveler, represented supreme solar consciousness, similar to Odin of the Vikings. A Votan glyph exists near the ruins in Tonina, which could be conjunctive proof of a Viking presence.

We can't see a burden of proof, just a glimpse into what could be. That glimpse is located in nearby Bachajón, a Spanish mission town where half of a stela depicts Votan.

An old book, written in the seventeenth century and called the Probanza de Votan, describes a family within the Tzotzil Maya who claimed to be descendants of Votan. He followed the lineage to a small town south of the city San Cristóbal de las Casas. Palenque is linked to many sites in the region, and most of them have statues, glyphs, and incense burners with depictions of men with beards.

Why don't archeologists consider the possibility of ancient sea migration? Because they are afraid to rock the boat. If they did, we wouldn't see rapid changes in people's world view. Archeologists want to see more than proof; they want to see it all spelled out beyond the shadow of a doubt.

Speaking of shadows, out of them emerges a little-known essay. The shadow master of the underworld himself, Carl Gustav Jung, wrote it. In the essay he played with the ancient etymological roots of the name Odin. Odin was a mythical Norse (aka Viking) God of war, who hung upside down on the Ydrasil, or Tree of Life. The tree includes nine levels of hell that the mythical king passed through to learn the runes, the Viking alphabet that originated in Germany.

In ancient Germany lived a character of a similar description that went by the name of Wodan. Jung makes a good argument for all of these names being one and the same. In Bachajón, in Chiapas, Mexico, we see the Glyph of Woh, which is Votan. In Palenque the number nine is a central theme of the underworld, which gives, at the very least, a chance to use mythology and numerology as a framework for transformation through symbolism.

Most rulers in positions of power practice a form of magic to legitimize their lineages and their control of the population. It makes sense, then, that their attempts to immortalize themselves included ensuring a safe passage through the underworld. It could be that the legend of Odin was based on the life of a real person.

Since the descendants of the Tribes of Judah displayed the Tree of Life in their artwork, and on stela five in Izapa and on the tomb of Pakal we're shown perfect examples of the Tree of Life, wouldn't the Mayan civilization have been primed for a Viking arrival of people who embodied the exact same Cosmo-vision? In Chichen Itza, yet another relatively unknown concept was painted on a mural where warriors were sacrificing red-haired, fair-skinned men, and cutting out their hearts. This mural was created in the Late Classic period, in the ninth century, right around the time of the end of the Viking civilization in Europe.

Comalcalco, a Mayan city of the same era, displays veneration to men with beards in its artwork. Located in southern Mexico in the Isthmus of Tehuantepec, which sports more beards in its ancient monuments then one would find in a Portland, Oregon coffee shop. These statues in the site's museum are seemingly from different time periods, Viking and perhaps Phoenician. I visited their museum in 2018 and took these photos.

Fig. 9 Viking lookalike statue in Comalcalco, Mexico
(Image courtesy of *Eli Coberly*, 2016)

Fig. 10 Phonecian lookalike in Comalcalco, Mexico
(Image courtesy of *Eli Coberly*, 2016)

It is reasonable to assume that the potential underlying unity beneath four cultural influences couldn't be just a myth. Even if they were, the potent symbolic message is clear. The cross and the Tree of Life within are a powerful geometric combination numerically aligned with the cosmos. It is as if we had been left a message of a tangible device that could be used for time travel into the abyss of the unknown subconscious and beyond.

The fragility of our existence is teetering on the edge of a world catastrophe, as we perpetually wonder what will happen next. Which state in America will have the next major shooting? Which country will lose thousands to a natural disaster? What world leader will put us in danger as a result of their own personal insecurities? When will the oceans become so contaminated, they become uninhabitable for most species? The short answer is that none of these possibilities is too far off, unless something changes soon. On the other hand, perhaps it is already too late.

For thousands of years the Maya were visited by many dynasties from around the world, as well as being exploited for their resources. They accepted their creationism repeatedly, because of the deep roots already woven into their cosmological vision. When the cross showed up at their doorstep, with a lingering memory of ancient wisdom, they accepted their fate. The Maya were destined to be a test culture in which the initiates learned of their own illusions through a story of illusion.

The triadic structures of the ancients were important around the world. It was through the energetic masters throughout history that we see manifestations of timelessness. Where better to represent this beauty than in the structures of Palenque? There is a correlation between the orientation of the architecture of Palenque and that of the Pyramids of Giza. Though the cosmic hearthstone concept was not limited to Palenque, they just happened to immortalize it through vastly superior art.

Punctuated equilibrium reared its beautiful head again when the cross group was built. Pakal I's son, K'inich Kan Bahlam II, initiated an artistic renaissance, revealing an ancient history long forgotten. This set the bar high for the opposition of a legitimacy created in the center of the cosmos, while posing interestingly potent yet new ideas not quite associated with the three gods. They were simply dubbed G1, G2 and G3. Bahlam II traced his ancestry not only to the beginning of the Mayan calendar, but also to the fire of the cosmos, where the Maya believed that souls are born.

18

SAN CRISTÓBAL

I arrived at the city of San Cristóbal de las Casas in Chiapas with an angry tailbone from a bumpy collectivo ride through the Sierra Madre mountains. I suppose to get to the bottom of things, one must sometimes exploit one's own. The city itself enjoys a mild climate for Mexico, due to its elevation (7,218 feet). The outlying areas produce some of the best coffee in the world.

I decided to sit for a time outside of a coffee shop. As I sipped the wisdom grown in the dust of the ancients, I channeled a long-forgotten memory. Two things often happen when I travel in Central America. One, I find myself in the right place at the right time for meeting the necessary people or finding the components to tell a synchronistic story. Two, there seems to always be some type of Catholic holiday in progress wherever I go, where the locals shoot off mortar type fireworks into the night.

To me, these types of explosions are worse than a 3 a.m. rooster crow, because, when they go off, I am reminded of when I assaulted fake bunker complexes during military exercises. My time as a paratrooper left my nervous system extremely sensitive.

Mexico has a history of explosive revolutionaries, starting way back with Emiliano Zapata in the early 1900s, and most recently the leader Subcommander Marcos of the Zapatistas. We might consider both to be the modern day, Central American equivalents of Robin Hood.

More drops of water slowly fall and ripple into the heart of an ocean as big as the universe, revealing the truth. The powerful forces that govern us have lied to the people. We have all heard that someone must lead, but the path of leadership can be a slippery slope. Men must rise and protect Mother Earth. It is time for us to listen to our sisters, wives, girlfriends, and mothers.

After hardly sleeping a wink from a mattress that seemed to attack my internal organs, I happened to wake up the next morning to a commotion in the hotel library room that was supposed to be available for study. It was a petition of local leaders, farmers, and a shaman for the ethical treatment of local resources. They explained the value of the entire ecosystem as a whole and highlighted the millions of years that humanity has been in the making.

The leaders projected a slide show that illustrated the dwindling forests and jungles in Mexico. Citing the four elements, a woman presented the concept that inert beings are those that do not have life. Another hidden reference to the five-pointed star emerged from the collective subconscious, without the messenger noticing from where it sprang. Most people want a solution to war. War is a crime against the people, causing destructive vibrations not only on the thread of humans as a species but throughout the entire web of the ecosystem.

Figure 11. Red five-pointed star
(*photoart985* via shutterstock.com)

I joined the party in the library and, in addition to the rest of the talk, we were presented with a piece of history that should not be forgotten. When the Maya of Chiapas became a commodity, the innocent people with one heart rose up and made a change under the guise of an incarnation of Votan. It was 1994 and with the enactment of the North American Free Trade Agreement (NAFTA) and behind his mask of humanitarianism stood Bill Clinton, presenting the idea that the market controls the price of goods. This system created a slave race once again out of the Maya of Chiapas.

When the Zapatistas went public under Subcommander Marcos, it was clear what they wanted. They were after fair payment for the farmers and crafters of the region. Why is it that the people who produce the goods can't do the bargaining? It is because there is no voice for them. With the Zapatista's Army of National Liberation, the heart of Chiapas had a voice. A rebel movement formed against the United States government's control over a puppet Mexican government.

So, the US supplied weapons secretly channeled through the CIA. The people took to the jungle where they were safe. This created a needle-in-a-haystack situation, during which troops began to crowd the streets and villages, interrogating the women and children.

They demanded to know where the Zapatistas were, and if they didn't answer, the women were often beaten and raped. This was done for our cheeseburgers, cheap coffee and fruit.

It got so bad, the people who weren't fighting began to protest the military occupation. And then a complete and utter tragedy occurred. Forty-six people, mostly women and children, were killed. Eventually, social justice warriors like Zack de la Rocha of the rock band Rage Against the Machine created awareness. The global women's rights organization MADRE stepped in, and the heart of the people spoke through the messenger, but no one shot them.

Even today, if you travel in the Sierra Madres, you could be subjected to a semi-non-violent traffic stop. The locals drag out homemade spike strips made of two-by-fours and nails attached to ropes and demand a few pesos per car or bus. The distinctions between the acceptance of violence in various cultures are remarkable. Justification has occurred since the dawn of agriculture, giving way to mass genocide in its many forms. But fortunately, another force is at work. This force is the divine play of the cosmos, creating balance whether we like it or not.

The end of 2018 marked the completion of an old way and the embodiment of the Aquarian age. In one week, the world saw a new Mexican president and the death of George Bush Sr. In the past we weren't given the tools of consciousness, because the resurgence of mass agriculture demanded a position of ownership and control. Control of the earth has ultimately usurped the wombs of women everywhere. War in the hearts of men has led to the demise of creation. Ironically, the creation story we follow is based on the fear of losing control.

Interpretations of Sumerian text in Babylon by Zecharia Sitchin and other ancient alien theorists preach fear of some sort, while reveling in as many unknown facts around the world as possible to prove the point that we are an experiment. I maintain that everything is an experiment.

If the soul is immortal, and the awareness of that immortality can be actualized in a single lifetime, what's the point? Who cares if the gods are real or not? The most real thing that can be agreed upon is the concept of a soul or an afterlife. Which begs the question: if you are afraid of death, why not prepare for it? And I'm not speaking of accepting Jesus in your heart, as prescribed by religion.

The most ancient of symbols are a map for collaboration in this new opportunity for actualization. Everything is now pointing to sacred geometry, mathematics, and tone.

A human body possesses thirty-three spinal segments and thirty-two teeth. In the Sri Yantra there are sixty-four connecting points plus the center, which equals sixty-five. It's called the bindu. Then add the spinal column, aka seven chakras. Add these all up and we see the number seventy-two. If you multiply seventy-two by two you get 144; and if you multiply that by three you get 432 — the number some say is the frequency of water. Four plus three plus two (432) also equals nine.

In Mayan cosmology, nine is the number for the underworld, and I believe this is the sacred equation tonally in its totality. There are many places on this great earth where art supersedes industry, and where expression of the heart is the foundational core of existence. These portals to other dimensions of expression can shine as a beacon of faith in the unknown. The choice is a constant dance of what in the Vedic tradition is known as the Lila, or "divine play" of Maya: illusion.

By contrast, at times we can revel in the darkness to cut through the illusion of ego. No one soul is exempt, and no one person can find his or her way to the center without participating in this play of illusion. When meditation is practiced, whether through painting, music, dancing, or even the focus of the mind to draw near to the heart, we can dissolve all illusion. When we can do that, even for a moment, we have arrived at nowhere.

This is exactly how the Maya stepped beyond time to view it as cyclical.

We can use the holy device of the Sri Yantra for the same purpose: as a portal of timelessness. It encompasses a feeling, a vibration, and a mathematical equation that leave room for all personality types and all walks of life. For the skeptics calling this dogmatic, imagine a world free from discrimination, racism, sexism, and war. The moment in our youths when we are taught to compare is the moment we forget.

This is also why psychedelics played such an important role in culture, pre-agriculture. They were used in ceremonies everywhere, in great astrological transits like the equinoxes and solstices. Once a line of comparison was drawn, we were torn between the masculine and feminine aspects of our hearts.

Modern yoga expresses manifestations of intrapersonal work in order to balance the highway of light (or serpent energy) as a journey through the chakra system. This system starts at the root of the spine and travels up to the brain through the entire spectrum of the rainbow, with each energy center. When a pure light shines through the shadow of illusion in each energy center, a true expression of its color can be seen. At this juncture it is up to the individual to sink or swim with the info being transmitted, to make a choice to learn from the illumination.

This awakening oftentimes comes with an unwinding in the physical body, harkening the reason for the popularity of the physical practice of yoga in the West. The beautiful thing is that each body of light is different, and each full expression, like a lotus flower, blossoms in its own time. Any forcing of this process would further the illusion of mastery.

When the full spectrum of the rainbow is achieved through an inquiry into parts unknown, then the tree is mature and the fruit ripened to perfection. This is not to say that humans aren't a perfect design. It is just that our species needs fine-tuning. It's as if our hearts form one string on a harp, but we are also part of a grand symphony. So, we take the time to fine tune the instrument, to get an ear for the part we play. While some of us need time to develop an ear for the perfect pitch our soul desires, others pick it up right away.

When we talk about the physical body, logical thinking comes in handy. Each chakra corresponds to an organ or a set of organs. A correlation is quite considerable and plausible in the yogic concept of the nadis, which the ancients say numbered 72,000, half of 144,000. If seventy-two points are in the Sri Yantra, including the Bindu and the sushumna nadi, which run through the center of the spine, then being a clear energetic channel is of utmost importance for the soul to actualize immortality.

The nadis are tube-like channels or portals of energy, where prana (life-force energy) travels through, connecting us to the infinity of the cosmos. This is Akasha and this is the space for the true soul, the atman.

19

THE FLOWER

Because it hasn't been scientifically proven, serious attention has not been given to precognition. When most people have these types of experiences, there is room for interpretation. A lot of the information is fragmented or metaphorically encoded. The information that comes through is different for many. Some might have a dream of driving and see their car run a red light. The next day they wait a little longer, for when the light turns green, only to see another vehicle run the light, drive through the intersection, and cause an accident.

These types of scenarios can lead to one questioning the nature of reality. The very fabric of what we thought possible changes. On the flipside, awakenings of a spiritual nature aren't always mountaintop epiphanies, unexplained lights in the sky, or meeting a guru in India. Sometimes simple everyday un-extraordinary events can lead to the biggest discoveries. It is a lack of planning or of over-planning that leads to a less rigid viewpoint. The point is: be flexible. Messages can come from the divine in the strangest ways. This is probably why the spiritual camp encourages folks to let go of expectations.

After a few days in San Cristóbal, I felt sick and exhausted. I left for Tuxtla Gutiérrez. The regional museum for Chiapas archeology has the earliest record in Mexico of the Mayan long count to date, starting in the year 36 BC.

I showed up on a Monday only to find the museum closed. Rather than banging my head on the stone carving around the corner from where I entered, I observed the carving closely and caught my breath. What I saw there was the five-flower glyph, the very symbol in meditation that had led me to that point.

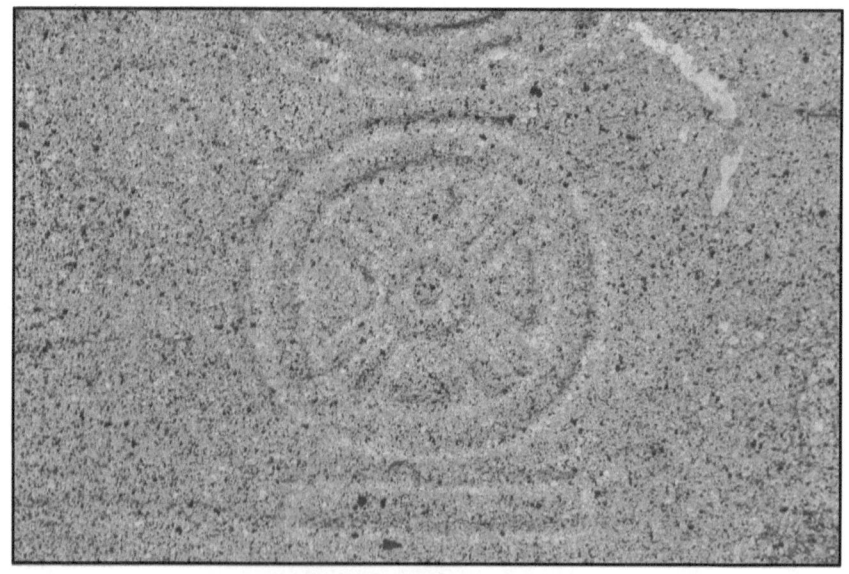

Fig. 12 The Five Flower Glyph
Regional I.N.A.H. Museum Chiapas, Mexico
(Image courtesy of *Eli Coberly*, 2016)

I reflected, thinking that war represented a point of origin for the rise and fall of civilizations. When men decided to grow crops, they saw the need to stake ownership of land, which created a paradigm shift in consciousness. Control of Mother Earth was symbolic of a need to impose control over the womb, which catapulted a need to defend a false sense of ownership.

We've imposed a deep ethical dilemma, resulting in a violent backlash lasting for thousands of years. It created our belief in time as linear and wiped out the ways of the ancients, who practiced time as cyclical and saw the need to keep track of gateways or portals. Clearing out history through conquest, men also erased the ancient practice of sacred geometric actualization through frequency. Biblical scholars adapted the story of Eden, because men feared the power of women's ability to create and connect with these ancient ways.

The serpent was, at its core, a sexual energy used for manifestation, and the fruit was Akasha. Now, through timeless symbolism and a change in consciousness, we can think for ourselves and repiece (not rewrite) a history that created war in the hearts of men.

I spent the next couple of days vomiting profusely and shaking in a hotel room. I cursed the glare of the day and ignored the room service that was brought to me. Two meals a day stacked up near the door. The partially inspected food, kept warm under saran wrap, festered. So did my mind.

I felt death creeping in and began my meditation practice. It was probably the sickest I'd ever been, but I decided to let it ride and to delay medical treatment. In between glimpses of spiritual enlightenment, I hacked up a lung or two. Ten years searching for the Maya, and all I'd gained was this near-death virus and additional confusion.

The next day, at 4 a.m., I barely fell into a cab, weaving down the streets, dodging wild Shepherd Poodle hybrids and garbage piles stacked twenty-feet high. Afterward, shuffling into line with the rest of the human cattle, I realized that the vast majority wore toxic beauty products. My already spun-out head felt squished by poison. I felt defeated.

"Help me, someone," I said.

Probably because I wasn't speaking Spanish, no one noticed. I fell forward and a security guard caught me. The quest for knowledge had left my body depleted and once again near death. He supplied me with water and a horse pill. Seeing double, I swallowed it and cleared TSA, slumping in agony into the nearest corner. Eventually, I made it stateside.

It was now 2020. Another two and a half years had passed. I sat and waited for a sign, a revelation about this flower. Why a flower, and why a star? How were they related? Staring at blank pages, empty spaces, and ghost towns, I noticed something. People were experiencing grief and the trauma of loss. They were suffering from feelings of unworthiness and shame.

But of course, everyone knows this. Most trauma of this sort manifests quicker in these days of expanded consciousness. Thanks to the Internet, we have info crammed down our throats and spewed out to anyone who will listen to what may or may not be the truth or fact, according to science. Mass confusion rules our society now more than ever.

We are enlightened yet enslaved. We are free but muzzled; for in the first quarter of the year that should represent "perfect vision," a calamity came to pass. The muzzling of society with the

Covid pandemic brought war to a culmination. This disease is a much greater plight than the overall deaths of our precious family members on this great earth. It is a war on consciousness, using our fear of death to implode expression and connection.

The year 2012 was a cosmic initiation related to how we love, what true love is, what internal war has done for the collective, and how we connect in relation to the masculine and feminine within. That year, on June 5, we saw Venus go retrograde and eclipse the sun. It is as if the collective feminine said, "It's time to stop. We have seen the opposition of feminine wisdom for the last two thousand years, and this unbalanced approach to life will never work."

What I see is a cycle that the indigenous peoples predicted. Venus was, and is, the key to predictions of war as a necessity. It is almost as if the people in power have no other option but to go to war when this type of transit is in play. The fascinating thing is that every time the five-pointed star shows up in art, we see a crippling of the feminine that is to be corrected. As it was with Subcommander Marcos.

The eight-year cycle of Venus creates an eight-petaled flower pattern. When this occurs, a five-pointed star forms in the center. Eight plus five is thirteen, which is a sacred feminine number celebrated by indigenous women worldwide. In essence, we see a sacred numerical balance between war and peace expressed infinitely in the cosmos.

When a star appears in the center of the path of Venus, in a retrograde fashion with a solar eclipse, we experience a major shift in global consciousness.

Just as distrust soars at an all-time high among the people whenever a black man is killed by a white cop in America, the world watches as the height of the dark masculine manifests its destiny of a dying system. Visions of a nomadic Mad Max society swirled in my consciousness. As a result of these unsought images, I knew that America would burn this time, and that finally, because of the worldwide web, no one would be able to hide out of ignorance. If you live long enough, you'll have the opportunity to upgrade and fine-tune your karma where it has been affected by your past decisions.

In ancient Teotihuacan, the rulers planned war to coincide with the times of Venus retrograding. Nearly two thousand years of relative time hasn't produced a major difference: consciousness has. Carl Jung wrote about the "shadow" as the unknown, dark side of people's personalities. In the year 2020, people acting from the impetus of their shadows casts doubts on the future of America and all humanity. The epidemic of the dark masculine manifested very clearly through Donald J. Trump, a paper-worshiping vassal lord for white men, who perpetually clutch paper dollars in their tight fists.

But paper burns in the end, leaving a trail of ashes and lies. What happens when power is stripped from the vassals of society? The people turn to rebellion, and a lotus of unfathomable beauty blooms from the mud as our entire species questions the past and stretches toward the future.

Around the same time that the United States rebelled, Elon Musk launched his private rocket into space and revealed his plan to merge man with machine. Neuralink is a high-bandwidth interface with the brain, in the brain. Elon looks to merge the limbic system and cortex in a new way, potentially enabling superhuman cognition and radically improving connection to information. The data flow rate will essentially be unlimited.

The user receives an implant via the removal of a piece of his skull. The surgical sight is then stitched up. Through this means, Elon Musk hopes to fix incurable issues such as quadriplegia.

Similarly, the ancient people of Paracas, Peru practiced trepanation: the act of cutting a hole in the skull. There are several theories regarding the original purpose of trepanation, but most argue that it was a medical procedure or ritualistic practice. The first record of this procedure is in Russia, near the Black Sea. The first Russian elongated skulls date back to around 5000 BC: the time of the great deluge recorded in the Bible. According to Brien Foerster's DNA tests, the Paracas skulls trace back to around this same period.

All the holes are located right on the crown of the skull, also known as the obelion point. Again, this is precisely where the sagittal suture is missing on the most famous Paracas skull. The ritualistic idea gives rise to interesting questions, such as: what kind of ritual was involved?

In mid-2019, I attended a lecture rendered by Brien Foerster and world-famous scientist Nassim Haramein. The room was packed at a sold-out UFO convention in Palm Springs, for they had advertised that they would be making a "special announcement." Eventually, after a lengthy and rushed presentation replete with scientific charts and graphs, they began to explain the results of a long-awaited DNA test on the Paracas skull.

Cameras flashed, hippies said "Wow," and the coffee I had drunk an hour earlier sought to shoot through my urethra. Dr. Haramein proclaimed, "We are happy to announce that the Paracas skull is formed of DNA not known to this world." Mr. Foerster went on to explain that this finding indicated he had discovered a new species: *Homo Sapiens Paracas*.

Dr. Haramein later chimed in that, "The skull evolved to get upgrades and grow."

Then suddenly, the event organizer, already upset because of the lengthy presentation, shut them down. I concluded that the scientist had found a new species that wouldn't receive much credit because, after all, skulls procured illegally by grave robbers and tested in private labs are of little interest. Given that there has been no breaking international news about a new species, I assume that no archeologist took the bait.

Recorded history starts around 4000 B.C. Anything taking place before that time could have happened in any way possible. Imagine a flood as described in the Bible, wiping everyone off the face of the planet. Why couldn't a few ancient neural-link-type devices be lying in the mud underneath the ocean, or even burned?

Why couldn't the flood have been for the purpose of wiping out the Nephilim (aka elongated skull) Angels? According to the Torah, the Hebrew translation for Nephilim is "Fallen One"; and these beings can be traced back to the Neanderthal period. The Israeli-Canadian investigative archeologist and film director, Simcha Jacobovici, suggests that these fallen ones are now extinct. It has been proven that, in the Levant area of the Middle East, Neanderthals and Homo sapiens mated, and that this interspecies joining continued for thousands of years.

The Torah suggests that proof of such has been found in the caves of Mount Carmel. As everyone knows, the Neanderthals became extinct. Possible reasons for this extinction include poor hygiene and social skills, and the lack of rudimentary crafting abilities.

So, who were the Paracas, and who were their descendants near the Black Sea in current day Crimea? Whoever they were, DNA testing has proved that they were not of Native American blood. This not only changes the history of South and Central American migrations, but it provides an interesting slant on the land bridge theory of the Bering Strait. It also crushes, once again, the notion that the first Europeans arrived in the Americas in the fifteenth century.

One of the oldest and most famous red-haired skulls comes from Spain, near the area settled by the Basque people. The origin of the Basque is thus far unknown. They have a unique language and a blurry history: not like the Bigfoot, more akin to the Paracas. And, according to the DNA test, the Paracas skull was not Neanderthal. Perhaps they were partially Basque. The mystery continues.

In 360 B.C., the Greek philosopher Plato told the story of Atlantis, a mythical island where man lived in harmony with nature. Here water was channeled to crops in all directions, and the gods merged with humankind. In the center of many circular canals stood Poseidon's temple, where the god dwelled and from which he ruled, with bulls worshiped and sacrificed in his honor. This was heaven on earth.

The people of that city were rumored to be half-man and half-god. The temple and shrines were covered with elaborate metallurgy of spectacular quality. Today, in Spain, certain mines up to five thousand years old still produce a red metal described by Plato. The locals call it "mountain copper" and it shines with an unusual luster.

Doñana National Park is a large mud flat in southern Spain. The area was studied by a team of scientists in 2019. Their findings were conclusive and lined up with every detail as described by Plato. There were even Ishtar-like goddess figurines collected from the surface that were carbon-dated to four thousand years ago, the time period of mythical Atlantis, making this expedition hard to ignore even by the most rigid of skeptics.

Another indication of synchronicity is a layer of methane, consistent with suddenly trapped organic matter, which lies beneath the surface at certain sites of this Spanish park.

In yet another layer, we see water. Because of these underground layers, the likelihood of Doñana National Park being dug up anytime soon is not very good. But there is a connection at another site just 250 kilometers away, called Cancho Roano. This large building, the equivalent of a small city, dates back to 550 BC. Not only was it a ritual city, which means it contained no housing and was devoted to religion, it was also a memorial city.

A memorial city is one that harkens to an earlier time through symbolic architecture. Cancho was built like Atlantis, with a moat surrounding the city. In its center was a sacrificial table sporting the ancient seal of Egyptian metallurgy consistent with the ancient Tarshish people of the Bible. These folks were masters of the sea, boasting the finest of ships and metalworking of any culture of their time.

Archeologists, like detectives in a murder case, steadfastly search for a smoking gun. Many aspire to find symbols etched in granite columns. Dr. Richard Freund, professor of Jewish studies and the "heavy" at this site, did just that. The symbol was exactly as Plato had described the place of Tartessus. The displaced exiles of antiquity needed a process of remembering a better time, when gods walked among men.

So many of them etched remembrances into stone, symbolically. And it's a good thing they did, because if we had to rely on the victors of war to preserve the truth, we'd be in trouble. After all, those who don't remember the past are doomed to repeat it in the future. Dr. Richard Freund never bothered to check to see who had made the circles he discovered at Doñana.

I suspect that if the late great Friar Diego Landa hadn't burned the entire written history of the Maya people, and if Julius Caesar hadn't burned the libraries of Alexandria, we would be able to piece together an airtight account of what really happened repeatedly throughout recorded history. But since recorded history was burned, we are forced to wait for the process of piecing it all together.

Many of the leaders back then were magicians capable of wielding the power of electricity through conductive symbology. Some were aware of their magic and others completely unaware of their role in the cosmos. It is said that King Solomon, the son of the biblical David, unlocked a magical seal.

Everyone was doing it . . . and everyone is still doing it today.

The leaders of the so-called Free World hide behind their powerful Twitter accounts to swing the population with yellow journalism and icon branding.

Venus completed her star pattern precisely when the protests began in June 2020. Then, after we'd had a glimpse of the end of America—bam!—a Penumbral eclipse took place. Eclipses, along with the cycles of Venus, have traditionally encouraged leaders to make energetic moves that have changed the shape of history.

Reaching back two hundred and forty Venus retrograde periods, a quite similar instance took place in Jerusalem. Rome invaded at the time of the solar eclipse and changed history forever, inciting a reason for a new religion and making a martyr out of Jesus. His philosophy would later consummate with that of the Roman cultural institution over the next 500 years, slowly birthing a bastard child: Roman Catholicism.

Five hundred years, galactically speaking, is the blink of an eye, but to us it measures around a dozen generations. Christianity took longer to take hold in Europe than the United States has been a country. The progress made in a few short weeks on the issue of police brutality in June 2020 encompassed more progress than that gained in the last few hundred years.

Fig. 13 The Pattern of Venus
(Image by *Peter Hermes Furian* via Shutterstock.com)

20

ALL AMERICAN

While confederate statues were torn down by protestors, more reform was wanted to literally dismantle the old paradigm. The people called for changing the name of the home base of Fort Bragg, one of our nation's toughest and most notorious airborne infantry units: The Eighty-Second Airborne Division. As a teenager, I joined the Army and eventually became a paratrooper in the 82nd Airborne.

I was fifteen when I decided to join. I remember walking into the high school lunchroom as a recruiter stood with a small card table full of pamphlets, which displayed tough-looking men with camouflage-painted faces. I looked at his face. It seemed even tougher: a square jaw framing a smirk. He had the thousand-yard stare they had talked about in all the war movies I had seen.

He introduced himself. "Hi, I'm Searnt Parker." I remember thinking, why not Sergeant? Later I learned that everything must be quicker in the Army, especially explanations. He told me that he was a sniper in a Ranger Battalion.

"What's it like?" I asked.

"What kind of things do you like to do, Coberly?" he fired back.

"I like to run and shoot guns. My friends and I go camping. We listen to loud music," I told him.

"You'll love the Infantry then. That's all we do. Here's my card. Call me next week."

In between then and when I called him to join, I did two things. First, I got my learner's permit to drive. (I was fifteen and a half.) And second, I looked at the front page of Newsweek magazine in the library. It showed the upper torso of a dead American soldier in fatigues being towed by a rope in the streets of Somalia. Apparently, a chopper had been shot down. I felt a jolt inside, and I decided right then that I was going to "make a difference." I begged my mom in the same fashion I did when asking for my tattoo the year prior. Eventually, she agreed to sign the release form. I wasn't old enough to drive and yet I joined the Army. Two years later, before I could buy cigarettes, I graduated from high school.

Three weeks later, on the Fourth of July, I found myself in downtown Seattle. I was sitting in a strange staging area of a hotel, set up for people joining the military. That night I walked across the street and watched the movie Independence Day on its opening night.

Later that month, while in Basic Training, I turned eighteen. After I learned to jump out of a perfectly good airplane, I was shipped from Fort Benning, Georgia, to Fort Bragg, North Carolina. (They bought me a bus ticket.) A year later our unit was shipped to Saudi Arabia in a cargo plane as part of a counter-terrorism operation.

Called Operation Desert Falcon, we were told that we were part of a much larger operation. We were perpetually guarding other Army units and Air Force personnel in a giant compound just outside Riyadh. It didn't take me long to notice that all the personnel we were guarding were doing paperwork. Hundreds of people doing paperwork all day long. For what? I wondered.

The compound itself covered about a square mile. Most days I was in one of six towers overlooking an airfield full of new F-14 Tomcat jets McDonnell Douglas had built for a Saudi prince. Directly to the left were some of the biggest cement oil tanks I had ever seen.

We rotated shifts, and one of our other jobs was searching vehicles entering the compound for weapons of mass destruction. Most of the vehicles entering were local men selling "Joe" Cuban cigars and gold chains, or Pakistani folks working in the chow hall. After the first few weeks of not finding any weapons of mass destruction in these strangers' vehicles, the novelty of fear wore off and I started to be nice to them. There were no weapons anywhere in Riyadh but ours, and we were there to protect the interests of America.

Occasionally, we would receive Top Secret information. For instance, that Osama Bin Laden had nearly been captured by US Special Forces. For me there was a pivotal moment when I lost my faith in what I was doing and what I had become.

I was shivering one morning at first light, staring out into the desert. I felt a jolt from my chin hitting my chest as I nodded off.

Then I saw a person running and making his way through the second strand of Constantine wire. Quickly focusing my binoculars, I saw to my surprise that he was one of ours: American Air Force. I got on the radio.

"HQ, this is Tower One. We have personnel in the wire; he's one of ours, over."

"Tower One, this is HQ. You have your standing orders."

I broke protocol and said, "I'm not going to shoot him."

One minute later, they told me not to shoot. I decided then and there that I did not believe in a system where protocol trumps humanity. Two years and many acid trips later, I was out with an honorable discharge. I left the Army before the age when I could legally drink.

As someone who has sacrificed years of his life for a false notion of freedom, I am glad to hear that the change of Confederate names of institutions are being considered by the consensus. However, I'm still concerned that whoever rewrites history this time will perpetuate the problem of the past but in the opposite direction.

21

THE BUDDHA

It is estimated that the Buddha was born around the sixth century, BC. His father was a mighty ruler of the Shakya clan in one of many kingdoms in India. The clan followed the ancient Vedanta philosophy, in which Vedic astrologers predicted the favorable times to marry, give birth, rise to power, or even to host parties. A dilemma arose when those same astrologers predicted that young Siddhartha Gautama, as they called him, would turn out to be either a great ruler or a contemplative.

The great one was born, and soon after, his mother died. His aunt raised him, alongside the king. They were so afraid Siddhartha wouldn't become a great ruler; they kept any hint of life's suffering from him. Old people in the kingdom were moved outside the palace. They went to further great lengths by also keeping all those who were sick away from him. Throughout his youth, the Buddha never knew the truth about death, sickness, and the poor.

Living in the lap of luxury in an opulent palace, Siddhartha was surrounded by beautiful young women who served him amid the backdrop of multi-colored lotus ponds. Just imagine his servants fanning him twenty-four/seven with palm leaves and feeding him exotic fruit. This was long before yoga became known as an exercise routine. Back then yoga was more about the sun, moon, and stars, which they saw as expressions of Brahman, the supreme God or ultimate reality.

A lesser reality came to pass when the powerful priests abandoned the philosophy and turned their religion into a business proposition. Siddhartha's father was in the rice market. His name meant "Grower of pure rice." But Śuddhodana was in for a rude awakening. His one true heir, Siddhartha, ventured outside the city.

There, Sid was introduced to the foreign concepts of disease, old age, and death. He became aware of the true state of suffering in his kingdom and in the world. That experience completely changed the direction of his life. He was destined, like Jesus, to make the suffering of the people his own.

Returning to the palace, he began to see the inconsistencies and lies of his father. He saw the terrible costs of war. In time, he exposed every injustice in the kingdom. He rooted it out where he saw fit, starting with the Brahman priests who were in the habit of taking a large percentage of the rice crop. They had created a monopoly ostensibly based on God, religion, and meditation, and had charged a fortune for it. Siddhartha challenged and changed things, but soon after that he left the kingdom behind, including his beautiful bride and his son. His father's plan had backfired.

Siddhartha was on the fast track to self-inquiry and sought out a secluded place. In his meditations, he delved into the depths of fire and water, neutralizing them. Wandering the earth, he punished himself, trying on for size the old ascetic techniques, but he found that they only created more suffering. His goal was to remove suffering in the world, not to increase it. He was radical, and many people considered him fanatical.

He had the audacity to challenge an interpretation of religion based on the holding of wealth, where people could purchase salvation. After becoming the Buddha, his transformative version of religion, based on inner enlightenment, spread to the far corners of Asia, and eventually, to the entire world.

The nature of this universe is duality, and it is the nature of men to be war-torn. Since the beginning we've had to be the tough one or the protector: the rock. That fire rages in the hearts of men, and an autopilot warlike switch evolutionarily takes over for most, but not for the actualized or aware. What happens when society has no compassion or time for those unaware of their unconsciousness? What happens when information moves quicker than consciousness?

Men are now expected to come from a consciousness that supersedes or speeds up our evolutionary growth. In response, some have turned to shaming, killing, or stealing from the established inequity. It's where we now stand in the mid-2020s. Racist white men became confused as the statues that their fathers had put up in order to keep order among the enslaved and poor black men in the city were taken down at the place where another man was shot. These are extreme examples in extreme times.

For me, the most extreme of all was when I learned that my old Army unit had been sent out to quell protesters. It was rumored that they had orders to fix bayonets (the practice of "fixing" a large combat knife to the end of a rifle). People were shocked, and the media had a field day. What could cause them to be so heartless? How could they do this? In the late sixties the Ohio National Guard was deployed to Kent State University in Ohio, where they fixed bayonets. People died not by the bayonet, but when the nervous soldiers fired on the crowd. Sad how quickly people forget recent history.

When a bayonet is fixed, it is with the intention of using it, and the 82nd Airborne Division is highly trained in fighting with a bayonet. For this reason, most of the time the 82nd gets turned back around from its deployments before it arrives. This division trains constantly and rarely gets used for its purpose, because most people surrender while the troops are en route, courtesy of their reputation.

When an out-of-balance male feels threatened, he tends to use whatever he considers his biggest threat to others. The best thing we can do is teach young men and boys what a real threat is. Most Type A personalities are matching an energy they feel but cannot articulate. It's something that just isn't taught to men. But schools and communities could be places where masculine and feminine are not limited to sexual preference or orientation.

In society we conjure ideas through a consensus. In all actuality only around 55 percent of the population votes. This leaves the morals of 2.5 percent of actual voters in the country to be bought. The swing of universal approval in America is monopolized, monetized, and all done under the radar; except that now people are conscious of this exploitation.

If we have ever lived in a simulation, then 2020 would be the burden of proof, standing tall. Humans don't want to be human anymore: they want perfection. Machines and artificial algorithms have sold out the flower of the soul. Handfuls of white, privileged men have changed the world; now, it spins in sync with the most popular likes and screen time.

The mostly male computer programmers of Silicon Valley decided for an entire generation that approval based on looks and popularity is more important than self-worth. This commonplace fallacy is robbing young men, and especially women, of their self-esteem. If you say, "Well, unfortunately, that has always been a part of society," think again.

For the past million years or so, most people had to seek the physical approval of others within a much smaller group for procreation. Now, if a young woman posts a photo of herself, she is subjected to unsavory comments from around the world. This context is not limited to the cyber world, which offers artificial characters online to entice young children and teenagers to stay engaged in device screen time.

These young "geniuses" are programming the future of our children's demise. If our children are the future, we are destroying it. The attention distraction model, coined by Tristan Harris in the documentary *The Social Dilemma*, explains the psychological techniques used by programmers to run algorithms that erode the fabric of morality.

Social media has instructed young people that the opinions of others aren't valid if they don't follow the allegorical lie subject to whatever is the best way to create funds for the CEOs of monster companies.

These companies are now the new gods, the new religion. There is a small window of time in which we can steer the course of humanity away from an all-out war on our sons and daughters. That war was initiated long ago, when another small group of white men decided the fate of an entire race and civilization.

I'm not sure if decades ago the FBI or CIA, formed by some of the most controlling men in the history of the world, could have imagined that they could steal the likeness of every human in the world, and that every person would become a commodity born into slavery. What must've been more surprising to them is how a worldwide investment in an allegorical social media platform could sow mass chaos and polarity within society.

Dictators are currently buying, bundling, and selling the futures of human stock. The image of everyone is being stolen and influenced for change in a manner ideal for the business of extinction. In the process, the dictator willing to pony up the most cash to Facebook is granted the power to dismantle entire countries' infrastructures. Just imagine a world where our children are free from apps that create false identities. Humanity isn't about procreation anymore: it has become about its opposite.

Our world's commodities have been exhausted, our children exploited—and now they are angry. In World War I, America's military introduced PSYOPS, short for "psychological operations." Well before the invention of the computer initiated the first social media in modern history. America, like most other great civilizations, nurtured a symbolic ideal of righteous colonialism. This ideal would shake the fundamental existence of every human to reincarnate.

With social media, everyone can be someone. We have a platform, as well as a voice that has longed to be heard and expressed. Yet our virtual expression is just that: virtual. The highest bidder has uniquely programmed our identity. This war-torn world is tired, and the people who have evolved to rule and lead have the power to change. The tree of life demands this change. Otherwise, we will perish like so many other civilizations before us. Now things are the way Artificial Intelligence demands them to be for maximum profits to the business professionals running the machine.

Opportunities have emerged digitally for our children to reveal their bodies and faces in exchange for money. The faces of our youth have been stolen, but not in the manner immortalized by The Grateful Dead, the iconic rock band that came up with a symbol to illustrate the loss of ego through LSD. It was called literally a Steal Your Face or, in other words, a "stealie." The symbol is a skull with a lightning bolt on the forehead. The skull represents one's consciousness, and the lightning bolt, an activation of such. I would suggest that this is the same symbolic message that spoke through the Buddhist tradition as the Vajra Essence.

Just as many faces or identification of egos were stolen for the consciousness of America's youth through the exploration of LSD, so has the social media agenda in Silicon Valley. Back then it was used to disrupt the function of society, and it served a just purpose for the expansion of consciousness. As I have said before, oftentimes consciousness can and does arise from the darkness. We know that dictators skilled in magic, dark and light, arise in the public eye and send ripples in the time-space continuum.

Now that this is in the forefront of consciousness worldwide, there is certainly an audience for rapid change and radical transformation. I believe that the code for unlocking the ancient secrets of comfort with death and immortality is available from a conglomerate of ancient traditional wisdom. One means for the masses to actuate it is with the sacred Sri Yantra, which is nothing short of a template for our individual light body to serve the great wheel of karma in the way we choose. And that choice is represented in our relationships. It is the great teacher of humanity.

Which is it going to be: fear or love? How can we use both of these emotions to discover the truth, to open the realm of new possibilities through other dimensions previously unexplored? If our bodies are, in fact, the Sri Yantra (or holy device) mathematically and tonally, then it should be possible for us to explore time. When the Sri Yantra is superimposed to scale on the human body, its center appears to rest on the third chakra. With this in mind, it makes sense that a healthy self-esteem is essential for transformation.

The transformation I speak of is one that stops a karmic metaphorical pattern the ancient yogis called Saṃsāra, the cyclical wheel of suffering through death and rebirth. It was written that if a yogi were to eradicate his samskaras—karmic patterns worn in the mind like grooves in a record playing over and over—he could be free from the wheel of Saṃsāra.

The moment before any choice is made is when the mind becomes prey to previously related trauma. All it takes is for the mind to equate a previous experience with a current one. In other words, right before dealing with a situation our inner senses will judge our experience with the same prejudice as the original event that reminds us of this one, and that prejudice will lead us to react, for example, in an overly cautious way. That moment in time has shaped who you think you are up until now. Every action you have ever initiated has literally been a reaction out of love or fear.

If, as the Maya described, time is cyclical, then the illusions of our senses can be appropriated to much more balanced responses, which would in turn relax the nervous system that connects us to all things. Meditation allows for this process. It is an inquiry, through sense withdrawal, into every thought and action you have ever conjured. We are talking about healing generational trauma in this life or in previous lives. Starting in this life allows a practitioner to get used to the concept. Just imagine a circular chakra spiraling, as described in the yogic tradition: at its center it expands infinitely and connects with all time and space.

I have figured out a way to time travel. Not to the year 1985 as in the movie Back to the Future, but rather through the chakras and tuning into their history. You see, if each chakra is a spiral and is connected through the nadis to everything, then time is just a wavelength of vibration that can be accessed by following those spirals energetically.

I began to travel this way in meditation and in my dreams. I realized that I could receive messages from my higher self, and from my inner child, trapped in his own illusion. I even received the age I was the first time I was shut down emotionally.

When we are told that we aren't enough and we hear it often enough, we start to believe it. But the root cause of our suffering lies on the bottom floor of our metaphorical house. The human fetus starts out round, sexless, and free from conditioning. As the growth process develops, a baby begins to open physically from the navel and the core concept of self-starts. Not only that, but the chakras open simultaneously, and the spine begins to form and the body grows.

But time goes by and people start to tell us who or what we are. The sad thing is, we believe them. And along the way our subtle energy that was tuned to recognize the totality of our actions becomes out of tune. Then, we react from fear. This takes place through social experiences with our family, friends, and peers, and it prevents us from having a full life experience, from taking calculated risks that encourage growth.

It is feasible to find the center by taking back your power and by returning to a healthy place of discernment.

22

THE CROSSROADS

We have become an instant-gratification society. Silicon Valley's super computers and Artificial Intelligence created a monster that initiated the biggest instance of punctured equilibrium since the Spanish arrived in the Americas.

On the tailwind of this, society has become more involved in people's day-to-day lives, and the organizers are the very ones who destroyed the previous structure. Only this time, in the year 2020, the world saw something different: an opportunity to transform the way we think and feel.

The flipside is that those behind such change bear the potential for being responsible for the US retrograding into a third world country. Like the rest of the world, we now see poverty spilling into the suburbs. Schizophrenia and drug use are at all-time highs, and so is homelessness. We could have focused on removing the root cause of suffering. Instead, in order to save time and trees, we created a paperless society and launched a digital one. And we left the power to a few men who could use the electrical force of their being to change the world in a positive way, if they wished.

Ironically, it comes to some as a surprise that we have antiquated human connection. Our souls have been sold to the highest bidder, like hogs raised for a Cedar Rapids slaughterhouse, and now we are witnesses to a shit storm of unholy practices. This time there is no traditional bloodletting, like that of the Aztecs or the Maya, no human sacrifices like the Celts and Egyptians. But the essence of these practices lies in the form of digital manipulation.

Just 2.5 percent of the population has been bought and sold to corporations in an effort to make more money by the minute for the ruling class. We could shift the scope from corporate logo worship of Facebook, Instagram, and Tinder back to the veneration of the Sun, Moon, and Stars. We can create a digital society in which we put Mother Earth and the universe first. This projection is an algorithm of what is best for Mother Earth, not business.

One problem with revamping the world is, if we follow that path, we will see the displacement of workers, families, and entire generations. Many people are dying already from the exigencies of our current inequalities. Diseases and natural disasters are the result. We only have so much carbon matter and energy. There is a balance to be found, and without war and disease, the human population would be recycled as carbon much more quickly.

Trees are carbon scrubbers that take in CO_2 (greenhouse gasses) and produce oxygen. They are the filters and bioindicators of mankind's mistakes, all rolled into one. If a tree falls in a forest and no one is around to hear it, does it really make a sound? Yes, it does, absolutely, because physics are in play.

The fall of humanity, as described in the Bible, has taken place many times. The Aztecs predicted the end of a fifth sun. The Navajo predicted the end of the fifth world. The reason why they knew about such catastrophes was through oral and recorded history. In their traditions, and in virtually all the others, it was written that, at some point, the sun would go black. The five-flower star glyph represents a form of gambling. It's as if they were saying that everyone using this five-pointed star would be rolling the dice.

The star, as I mentioned before, is missing the feminine aspect of the energy of the symbol, as manifested over millennia with five worlds, five points, and four directions with a center. The Pentateuch consists of the five chapters of the Old Testament, and it describes the rise and fall of humanity.

Really, all that comes through this big elaborate story of lineage and human mistakes is a reason to await another messiah. The Jewish people of Israel in the present are ready to build a third temple that unites the people. They believe that the Dome of the Rock is the original site of the great Temple of Jerusalem, the second version of which was destroyed by the Romans. It is common knowledge that the Jews are waiting for something to happen.

The Dome of the Rock is built on a great platform measuring thirty-six acres. It is constructed in part of large rocks weighing several tons, and on one side, known today as the Wailing Wall, you can see where people put notes containing prayers in the cracks between the rocks. King Solomon the magician, son of

David, was the one to initiate the energy of the five-pointed star that eventually became six.

Many Christian and Jewish scholars agree that the holiest of holies never stood where the Dome of the Rock is. Josephus, a Roman-Jewish historian, gave detailed accounts of water standing on the site where the Second Temple was built, after the First Temple had been destroyed by Nebuchadrezzar II of Babylonia. Also, he and others described the Tenth Roman Legion as dwelling in housing, not tents.

Most, if not all, of the Roman outposts of this nature spanned thirty-six acres. The current supposed site of the holiest of holies is not even where the Muslims built the dome. After the conquest of Jerusalem, the Romans built a platform in a prominent location towering over the Jews. Later, the Muslims acquired the world's most disputed piece of real estate, built in the old location.

The essence of alchemy, as described by Carl Jung, is a transcendental function that brings together the disparate elements of the conscious and unconscious minds. If trauma is stored in the chakras, then change comes through actualizing the moment of togetherness. In this realization, time becomes a process and a practice, as opposed to something weighing us down until death.

The ancient peoples of the Americas were no strangers to natural disasters. An account of a mass exodus from Central Mexico is recorded in the Boturni Codex of the Aztec people, which details through pictures and text their population leaving a pyramid and traveling by canoe to another place. The fact that this destination induced native peoples to wear furs indicates a location somewhere with cold nights and north of the equator.

A conglomerate of accounts including the Popul Vuh, the Chilam Ballam, and other remaining codices confirm spiral-like patterns of migration. Many confirmed spirals are located around the world. Also, the spiral migrations of the Aztecs are illustrated in the Borgia Codex. Their canoes likely washed up on the shores of Florida before they wandered north to Georgia.

Among these accounts, the same words, art, and story are illustrated clearly, as are the farming techniques, building methods, and historical names. At the settlements close to modern day Columbus, Georgia, Blue Ochre was discovered. The same substance was recently found in 2020, deep in the cenotes of the Yucatan.

Worldwide migration has been and is recorded on rocks, monuments, structures, text, and orally, for at least the last five thousand years. The symbol behind this migration is a spiral, and spirals were found near the ochre in a "native American settlement."

The Hopi people of the American southwest claimed to emerge from the underworld. Their practice of using a kiva (or small stone meditation building) for divination is astonishingly beautiful. The individual or group enters the kiva. Here they wait until the solar rays are directly above, which happens especially on the winter and summer solstices. On the longest days of the year, the sun's path is directly overhead.

It is said that the hole in the center of the floor of the kiva symbolizes the point from which the first people sprang from a lizard-like existence to our current human form. This tiny hole in the floor, called the sipapu, is where moments of transference occur. Long ago, the knowledge of the animal world merged into the human psyche. The Hopi people were famous for their animism, like the Maya, Inca, and most indigenous tribes.

One petroglyph dubbed "Prophecy Rock" illustrates two paths, one of love and another of fear. Like the Hopi, most of our ancestors led their families through perilous journeys of migration just for a glimpse of freedom. They simply wanted their own piece of dirt and their own god. But they were willing to sacrifice it all just for a sight of what might be.

All Hopi crossroads come with a choice and a purpose: to go toward the path of healing for our planet through peace and love, or to give our sovereign power to technology and let it steer the ship to mass extinction through division.

23

PROPHECY

The Hopi, aka "the peaceful ones," wrote prophecies on rocks. It is now a matter of when, not if, the world will be flooded, and massive-scale casualties will result. Everyone everywhere has scribed art and literature about natural disasters and cataclysms. It is well documented in many of Graham Hancock's books, as well as those of Egyptologists and scholars.

The origins of symbols are shrouded in mystery, but the Hopi are the key to understanding a history long forgotten. Their creation story illustrates a white man coming from the east. The spiral and cyclical nature of the Hopi's migration documents a past linked to the Maya and Aztec peoples.

Migration-dominant cultures followed the constellation Orion. I believe they did this because there was something to the trajectory of the archer in the night sky. As with any kind of war, regardless of size or scope, we see assimilation of the subordinate culture. The Roman theft of religious beliefs, architecture and art, and the plight of the indigenous in North America, ebbed and flowed with Mother Earth's moans and groans.

Over tens of thousands of years cultures rose and fell, were assimilated and conquered, all the while re-using earlier symbols as if they had invented them. Hitler started the Nazi regime with the swastika fluttering behind a massive German machine. He, like other leaders, not only studied history and religion, but psychology. He knew that these powerful symbols had been used for millennia, that the swastika represented a potent combination of elements.

The Hopi employed the swastika symbol in their rock carvings, but the first to use it were the Tibetans. Bon pre-Buddhism is the oldest sect of religion in the Far East. As in the Bible, Buddhists had a funny way of recording years. Leaders exaggerated the time-length of events to make themselves appear closer to God. They even impersonated God himself.

It is written that the swastika, dubbed "Thung Drung", originated at the base of Mount Kailash, the birthplace of Shiva, some eighteen thousand years ago.

Some scholars date the swastika's origin back eight thousand years, and others more like five thousand. Many who translate the text literally maintain that the founder of Bon, an earth-based Shamanist religion, initiated it before all recorded history. I feel that since the swastika pops up around the world in so many time periods, it doesn't matter. The true embodiment of the symbol represents a timeless knowledge of immortality.

The knowledge of immortality is the collective journey of all traditions worldwide, and a perfect example of this truth can be seen in the Hopi. Where the Maya were masters of the illusion of time, the Hopi were masters of space. They were like the yogis of ancient Tibet and India. They sat in their kivas and downloaded history through the ether via the sipapu, the small hole I mentioned before that lies in the floor next to the fire hearth. This Hopi practice strongly resembles the hearthstone cosmology of the Maya. In addition, we see their similar fascination with the Orion constellation.

If the spiral and the swastika can be found globally to this day, and were first illustrated by the ancients, what does this tell us? I believe it cautions us to prepare to migrate, or to start inventing ways to deal with the melting polar ice caps. If it is all pointing to global warming, then like the Maya, we are almost too late. If we look at how many people are buying sprinter vans or retrofitting retired soccer mom vans, we can see that the migratory patterns have already begun. The average global citizen is fed up with the establishment's lies.

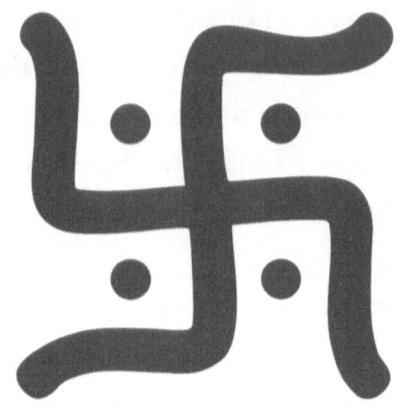

Fig. 14 Hindu Swastika
(Image by *Tudor Antonel Adrian* via Dreamstime.com)

In December 2020, I wanted to see these spirals, swastikas, and kivas for myself. I flew into Las Vegas and headed to the Four Corners—the perpendicular-bisected junction of Utah, Colorado, Arizona, and New Mexico—for a look-see. I drove all night to Winslow, Arizona. For some reason, when I arrived in town the Eagles song "Take it Easy" was playing in my head. I carefully looked around with hope, but there was not a flatbed Ford in sight.

My hotel was quite vintage, the walls plastered with modern art portraying heads of state and their weaknesses. I began to see that the swastika was often represented in Navajo and Hopi art. How did they know?

After consuming southwestern Mexican food, lots of it filled with chilies, I chugged some coffee and felt more awake. The breakfast waitress asked me about the purpose of my visit. I told her, "Looking for spirals carved in the rocks." She gave me directions to a place called Rock Art Ranch. So, I sped off down a dirt road to get a glimpse into the ancient past.

An old cowboy with one good eye and a meandering voice met me at the gate. He looked to be about eighty-five.

"I'm feeding my cattle," he said as he clutched a handful of hay. "Follow me to the barn."

I obliged and checked out his homespun museum of "artifacts," which featured arrowheads, pottery, and baskets.

His son walked up and said, "This is Dad's man cave."

"Cool, when can I see the spirals?" I asked anxiously.

"Let's go," they chorused.

I followed their beat-up ranch truck for a few miles, and a few cow patties later they stopped. We all got out of our vehicles, and they showed me a map of the canyon wherein the ancient Hopi had carved on a flat rock in the sand. We gazed down at what appeared to be an aerial view of a spiral connected to the river. Next to this were hand drawn images of several animals and perhaps some game, including antelope, sheep, and elk.

The design evoked in my mind a combination of a map of where to hunt and a partial catalog of what was available for food. But it also depicted a kachina: a dancer that connects this earth to another world. Many kachinas dance for water and this one certainly was.

The two men explained to me that their family had bought the ranch in the 1940s, and that their ancestors had settled land west toward the border of Nevada in the 1800s. We then drove off to the canyon.

They had a nice little viewing station for tourists, which

overlooked the river. The old man gave me directions. He said that if I followed the path down, I would see thousands of petroglyphs. I made my way down. Once inside the canyon I saw part of a map of ancestry that had unmistakably guided many others to the water and the hunt. I felt vibrantly alive. My mind slowed, and my heart felt a deep connection with the ancient Hopi. I felt the layers of their migration story of survival and creation.

Seeing more of the same, I traversed the mini boulders on the canyon floor. But something else caught my eye as the sun's rays provided a perfect play of light and shadow. Anthropomorphic drawings. My favorite was the lizard, or bug-looking character, with a human penis. This type of art was clearly an effort to connect and share the bridge between man and animal.

The next morning, I awoke refreshed. In my sleep, I had dreamed that I was in the parking lot of a coffee house, sitting in my rental car. I opened the door and a five-foot rattlesnake slithered by. Then my dog Penny, who had died years before, brushed up against me and spoke to me telepathically.

I'm okay, Dad, her thoughts whispered.

She pounced on the rattler just as I called her away. Then I awoke and sat up in bed.

Dreams are portals to other dimensions and bear a relationship with the infinite. Dreamtime, as taught by indigenous around the world, is an excellent means of communicating with the dead. We not only receive wisdom from beyond the grave but truth about the past, present, and future. The Hopi reproduced these types of states in the kiva through sensory deprivation, like the yogis of Ancient India.

I remembered the nearby Pueblo site of Chaco Canyon: a mass scale ceremonial center designed to shock and awe anyone approaching. The truth is that there is little to no evidence of this massive complex holding long-term residents. There were few burials and little decaying organic matter that would indicate either a food waste dump or human excrement.

Some of the buildings were constructed to line up directly with the sunrise at the equinox, and others with the moon. They were designed to immortalize a potent combination of creation. The powerful people in charge made this barren wasteland a Native American Mecca for the creation of heaven on earth. A spiral pattern on a rock is etched above the city, which during the equinoxes when the sun hits it is covered in half light and half shadow.

The moon has an eighteen-year cycle in the middle of which it lines up perfectly with the center of the city and the spiral on the rock.

This was the best and most potent time for the predictions of outcomes, and even influences on weather patterns. Here was a Mecca for ceremony and sound. Like the ancient site of the Göbekli Tepe temple in Turkey, the people here played with collective resonance. And, as in Turkey, we see T's in the architecture echoing the Tower of the Winds in Palenque, Mexico.

In Palenque, the T represents a wind the Maya called "Ik": fundamentally an understanding of the life force of air and wind that permeates creation; that which the Far East dubbed chi or prana.

Every culture planted a seed in the center of their known

universe that combined cardinal directions and the elements, which were and are the natural forces governing this earth. These natural forces were illustrated with mostly the colors of red, yellow, white, and black. The ancients left clues to the origins of our purpose here on earth. The people living in the American Southwest knew through the dreamtime that our purpose was to learn peace through these concepts. They knew that they had been tasked by the creator to unite all four colors of the human race for the purpose of eventual liberation.

The basic similarity of these three sites is not only in their mutual T's but in the way they took great measures to cover up and hide evidence. They sealed up entrances, removed roofs, and in the case of Göbekli, completely submerged the site.

Why cover them up?

Because the power was not actualized. It created earthquakes and lightning storms and sent vibrations deep within the earth. This happened in Africa, at Stonehenge, and around the world. They left subtle clues everywhere they wanted us to remember, so that when out-of-balance leaders gained too much control over the earth and its population, we might learn and understand before it was too late.

24

THE FUTURE

P sychedelics and music go hand in hand. Both are portals to the center of our known universe, especially when combined in ceremony. It happened on every continent and with all four corners of the human race. And the Four Corners region of Utah, Nevada, New Mexico, and Colorado was such a place.

The ingestion of Ayahuasca for transformation is a growing trend in so many circles. It took me more than five years to integrate my one and only experience, to the extent I have been able to integrate it. I am convinced that a growing number of people will harness a power similar to that of the ancients, in which they attempt to control their destiny in strange ways. Not like mutants among the X-Men, but something different.

Ayahuasca infiltrates your blood barrier and floors your serotonin levels, some say to such an extreme that impurities must come out. This happened to me. So much so that my soul left my body because my nervous system couldn't handle such a shock. I had received the Anthrax vaccine before being deployed to the

Middle East, perhaps it became toxic in my bloodstream.

I can still remember going toward the narrow pinpoint of light, like it was yesterday. Ever since that day when I entered deep relaxation after yoga or meditation, I suffered shaking sensations. At first the episodes were filled with more pleasure than I had ever experienced. But the days passed into weeks and months, and the shaking became more aggressive and longer in duration.

Most of the time I was embarrassed, as my chest would come off the ground and my neck would stiffen. It was as if I experienced what it felt like for women to orgasm. Then it started happening at random times, while I was waiting for a bus, or even while driving, and I thought, am I going to have to deal with this forever?

One day I met a guy who had studied with the same dream teacher I'd studied with. He gave me an exercise for grounding, as taught by that teacher. He showed me that, if I grounded the energy I'd been experiencing to Mother Earth, as if via a copper rod sent into the core of the earth, I could control the shaking. It worked, and I began to feel powerful again.

In November of 2020, I decided to visit Maui and connect again with the sweetness of her jungle.

For days leading up to the trip, I started to receive visions of that pinpoint of light. This time, though, it was different. I saw myself leaning up against the opening to the great mystery with a big smile on my face. I noticed that I felt comfortable there. I became curious as, each day, I saw my face in more detail.

I scheduled a massage with a friend. Halfway through, when she touched my face, I began to shake. She shrieked in fear that I was hurt, but I told her to continue, that I needed to work through it. She started to sing to me while playing a wind chime. It was the same wind chime, in the same key, they had used in the Ayahuasca ceremony, right before I temporarily died. Her music brought me back to the beauty of the visions, lessons, and messages I'd received.

After the session the therapist asked me if I knew what that shaking experience had been about.

She explained, "I've done Aya several times, and I had this experience of shaking, too. It scared the shit out of me." Her boyfriend had held her down, and it lasted at times for upwards of five hours.

"Well," I said, "it's a grounding process."

However, I believe most humans aren't ready for this type of serotonin rush, evolutionarily speaking, because we still don't know what Ayahuasca is, where the "grandmother" is, and what or who she is. Maybe she is an intelligent entity in the center of the earth. Perhaps she forces us to remember the hard lessons through a switch that disables some of us like a vehicle with a device that controls its speed. When the mind elevates in fear, then the nervous system burns out and the body shakes, because electrical charges fire where the chakra isn't firing on all cylinders.

Either way, it is probable that the energy uptake of humans in these ceremonial centers is too much collectively for the majority to handle.

This could be why Göbekli Tepe, Teotihuacan, Chaco Canyon, and many other sites were sealed and abandoned. The people became disenfranchised from their rulers, and the earth tired.

Nicola Tesla was conducting experiments in the mid-1940s

that sent ripples through the time-space continuum. In essence, he used mathematics and tone with a few modifications.

Whatever collective humanity is focused on will become reality. Regardless of politics, weather, or war, it will occur. We are powerful in more ways than we currently know.

So the question is: what are you focusing on, and how can you use your gifts that are uniquely you?

I have personally witnessed several occasions when people "called in Mother Nature" at these sacred sites. Sometimes she rumbled, and sometimes she showed us a rainbow!

Also, in the spiritual or religious arena, the more worshiping or practicing, the more powerful the practice becomes. In other words, humans are batteries with energy tanks in which, the more the lunar and solar energies (i.e., feminine and masculine) are combined, the more electrical charge a body possesses. This is why the US government, or a political faction, needs us to power the hate.

Our fate was decided long ago. This is our dharma, or purpose in life, as clarified by the Eastern Religions. One's dharma interacts with one's karma. Our karma is a result of our thoughts and actions in this life and others. If you add up all these concepts, practices of cultures globally, you have three, six, and nine. In terms of energy, this is one quarter of the Sri Yantra.

Scientist and Astrophysicist Michio Kaku is an expert in what's called the String Theory.

He claims that it is as if the creator of the universe were a musician playing the twelve musical notes in a grand symphony. We can learn a great deal from this.

So, the human body is a time-traveling, battery-playing symphony, conducting electricity with heaven and earth, designed to fulfill dharma. As if this weren't enough, we have to wade through the consequences of what our soul said and did ignorantly through another body. But wait, there's more.

Highly evolved Buddhists across the millennia have achieved what is called the "rainbow light body," when one is free from karma and needless suffering, and the mind is luminous and can focus on a pinpoint of consciousness at the time of death and beyond. Around forty days after a Tibetan yogi leaves this planet, dying consciously, his body shrinks in size—in most cases to the size of a baby, or even that of a fetus.

From the start, something happens to his soul as it passes through the dark tunnel or tube after death. The yogi is presented with choices along the way to distract him from the light at the end of the tunnel. This is called the "bardo" state. The distractions include wrathful deities, and even horrific monsters disguised as Dakini goddesses. If the soul of the person takes the bait, he is destined for more suffering.

At the end of the tunnel the practitioner is presented with a room full of copulating couples, engaged in all sorts of different positions and styles, some participating in conscious lovemaking and others even in violent sex. The yogi can choose whichever couple they wish to be reincarnated through in the next life. If they don't wish to reincarnate, they will likely achieve the rainbow light body. This is well described in the Dzogchen text.

Death happens sooner for some than for others. They see the struggles in life as just too great to overcome, so they end their own.

Many live with the pain of witnessing terrible events that have come to pass. War veterans are recipients of these sorts of memories.

Our DNA tells a story of struggle and transformation. The symbols of our consciousness have perpetually risen in art throughout time and space.

The Hopi indigenous people's creation story warns of the two paths. It incorporates undertones of Eastern metaphysical philosophy. Their story illustrates and draws upon the very essence of all spirituality and migration as told in recorded history. Lines are literally drawn by a spider creator, like Indra from the Rig Veda. The people are instructed to be in harmony with creation and nature. There were four worlds and all have one thing in common: humanity blew its chance many times before and this time is the last.

Here I sit on December 20, 2020, at the peak of darkness of the winter solstice. I bear the name of Elijah the prophet, who was an announcer of false prophets. Like other prophets, I happen to be exploring my gifts. My gift to you is that fear is a false prophet and unconditional love is the new religion. When you see that pinpoint of light in the darkness, focus on the center of your heart. Your ancestors and mine were all cut from one mold, from one creator. We will return to the light, all of us.

25

WATER BORN IN MUD

The best of the best will always be topped. The strongest will always fall. Every up has its down. You get the idea. Chances are, if you are a man or relate more strongly to masculinity, you historically project your self-worth and sense of identity into what you achieve.

If you're a woman, then you might be charged with the acceptance of your outward beauty or the care you provide for your loved ones. Obviously, this role is somewhat outdated, but its roots are strong—strong enough to remain present in the DNA in order to attract a mate.

With a rise in consciousness, creation is something that can be embodied without the necessity of sexual union. We can channel the energies of our sexual sublimation through our purpose and our art. Why spend the energy that arises within us as if it were a checking account? Many male tantric practitioners use the essence of their saved orgasms to create a world in which they wish to live. For the most part, men literally spit out their seeds that they've sown into a woman and create an image of how both parties project themselves in the world.

Padmasambhāva was not so ironically born in the eighth century. They called him the "Lotus Born" guru and the third Buddha. The number eight was his to embody and teach the world. He and his consorts engaged in "sexual union" with the divine, creating a healing so strong it was felt throughout infinity.

The Hopi were in a long line of human beings who migrated for water. They even used clay jars or vessel-like containers to locate it. They wrote through their petroglyph spirals the symbolism of their migration for water. One woman near Stonehenge named Maria Wheatley was gifted with a valuable skill, that the ancients knew of and practiced, called "dowsing."

Maria uses copper rods to locate water and vortexes of water. She also has located the graves of ancient elongated-skull high priestesses near her hometown in Marlborough, England. The skulls, along with others, were smashed in, some of them split ear to ear. Basically, a bunch of warring roundheads had wiped out the long heads.

As the Hopi explained in their prophecy of the second world, the longheads became too powerful by using their creation for vibration. They were also excellent metal workers, and polished stones to track water sources. Was there a flood? Or did the roundheads kill another species out of fear of the great power of the feminine and a matriarchal society?

Liberation through sex might be a risqué topic for some. (You know who you are.) But consider the ramifications of a society repressing a power that literally moves mountains, shakes canyons, and floods desert floors. This is what we are capable of, yet our leaders want us sitting in cubicles, sucking from straws and swiping screens.

If, according to the ancients, we are made of the stars, which are mostly made of water, then water is the key to the serpent vehicle device. Kundalini energy at the base of the spine is our ticket to ride the highway of connection to the Atma, the true self.

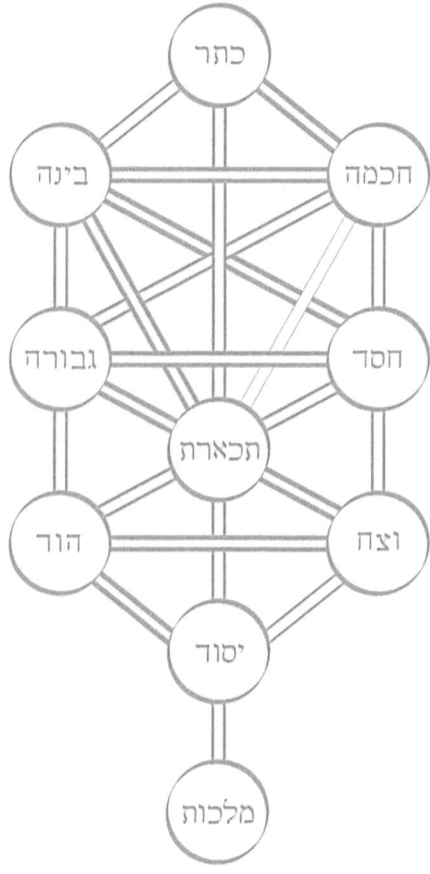

Fig. 15 Kabbalah
(Image by *Dreamsidhe* via Dreamstime.com)

In conjunction, the mystic writers of the Kabbalah described the concept of Ein Sof and the breaking of the vessels.

Ein Sof is the acknowledgment of the divine in the moment before the experience of it takes place. Like the first light seen of dawn in the east, we were destined to follow the water of creation in the moment. Humans were meant to migrate so that we would not forget creation.

Every ancient culture had a process of sacrifice. They broke pottery in Egypt, Europe, and in North and South America as an offering for the vessels of creation.

Another similar offering mentioned in Hinduism is Amrita. Translated as the "divine nectar of the goddess," it is said to be the fluid that flows from the spine to the sexual organs.

In every woman are two small glands located near the g (or Gräfenberg) spot, called the Skene's glands. (Of course, everything is named after the scientist who discovered it.) The Gräfenberg is stimulated manually with a "come here" motion. Then, with the proper mindset and combination of contraction and expansion, much like the universe, come the waves and the ocean of nectar.

This nectar can amount to liters at a time, and many women have described the moments when it arrives as a powerful, masculine-like energy of liberation, like nothing they'd ever felt before, as if they had been freed from generations of shame and guilt.

The Hopi said that the Creator destroyed the second world controlled by the longheads, who moved energy through the tops of their skulls. The roundheads wiped them out, which initiated the third world. They wiped them out because of fear. They were practicing the electrical uptake that I describe and their heads grew in length as they aged.

Now, in today's world, humanity has one more window of time for rectification.

The Kabbalah and the Hopi describe us as having this last opportunity to set things right. They both believe in the return of a messiah, and the Hopi believe that he will be a white man named Pahana. Every man and woman can be a magical messiah, like Jesus, for the feminine.

It is up to us to systematically remove the hatred that was necessary for us to live with in the past, so that we could learn now to embrace the future. Let the waters flood and the electricity flow through the highways of time and remove the chains that bind our DNA. Let the higher dimension of love be the new religion: our lives are depending on it, and our souls have been waiting for it.

December 2020: I was headed back from the Four Corners region, flying home out of Las Vegas. On the way I noticed a Veterans Memorial located at an ever-shrinking National Guard base in Belmont, Arizona. I couldn't stop the energetic pull I felt, guiding my car off the interstate to the cemetery that apparently contained 716 spaces for the dead, most of them Anglo-Americans. I pulled up to a procession of cars of people, waiting for a three-gun salute to commemorate the death of another man who had given everything so that others wouldn't have to.

In the distance, miniature American flags rippled in unison with the breath of the Great Mother. The final resting places of these veterans, who had served in wars since the inception of this Army base, were given the gift of a nearby snow-capped mountain. All I saw was a small attempt to give back to men who will never see again the camaraderie they had while serving.

I thought of my own robbed youth: the angst I've felt my entire life was encapsulated in this very weighty pinpoint of consciousness. The procession began, and I wept as I saw the name of the man whose ashes would be stored in this columbarium. I missed my old teenage friends who had been tasked to fight to the death beside me. Akasha, the central ether of the four directions, the blank spaces in the earth and these miniature white billboards awaiting many others to complete this cycle of death, birth, and war . . . in the hearts of men.

I blessed the four directions and thanked the three-thousand-plus Navajo and Hopis who worked alongside the Pahana to create a new earth. Those 716 spaces in total will eventually be filled at this memorial, on the very site that manufactured munitions to help win the war. The theft of the ancient swastika symbol helped complete the prophecy of Pahana and the fourth world we now reside in as the light returns from darkness.

I heard a voice say, "Everything you have experienced up until now has been a process of purification. The four directions will carry your soul's migration to its final resting place in the stars. After all, if you add up 716 with 4 you get 720: the number of bodies buried at this cemetery plus the four directions. And in the center is you."

CONCLUSION

I have shown a country with a violent past as a tributary of the world. America the great is a civilization founded on colonialist slavery and built over the mass graves of indigenous children. We have all the hallmarks of other recycled truths of the "great civilizations" embedded deep within the fathers of our great empire. In a perfect world, there would be no war and no trauma passed down to our children, who are not yet men and women.

The world isn't perfect, and evolution isn't always the best thing for one species. It is just evolution. This is simply defined as change.

Writing this book has afforded me a true depth I never would have had personally believed possible. But it did not come without cost or sacrifice. I am making some bold statements about history, religion and humanity. This has and will perhaps alienate me, but I believe that most of humanity will see this ancient science of universally galactic yoga, the joining of the sun, moon and stars in the heart.

Earlier in the book I mentioned the connection that the zodiac has with the ancient roots of animism, called the circle of animals, and that war has been a staple of the human experience since the dawn of agriculture. The circle of animals in Göbekli Tepe, Turkey is the beginning of agriculture, religion and most likely the point of origin in the creation story, Eden.

The circle of animals was represented in time and space in relation to farming and creation but shifted to language through color and tone. Tone was part of the great ceremony around the world while ingesting entheogens. Human sacrifice was just a part of this and, as a result, cultish behavior around death transpired.

Scholars and Archeologists of this pre-biblical site are now alluding to an ancient "skull cult." The same as the Aztecs' initiation of sacrifice of the Maya and the Nazca, and their head-hunting cult which wiped out the elongated skull people of Paracas. Nassim Harimen, an astrophysicist, says that the elongated skulls of the *Homo sapiens Paracas*, "Evolved to get upgrades and grow."

Around the world most of these skulls were smashed in or involved trepanation/brain surgeries.

The onlookers of this rare species must have seen the raw supernatural power developed by mostly the feminine. They wanted to kill them and claim their power. They feared the connection with heaven and earth. Then they emulated them with cranial deformation, infant headboards, etc. This began the end of the elongated skull species, into the times after Christ.

The Europeans who bought into Christianity traveled the world spreading colonialism. This crusade wiped out the memory of our entire race by destroying the evidence, while also globally consolidating the entire European religious experience as a business.

They decimated the concept of heaven on earth as originally actualized in Eden, Turkey, and made hell of the earth. Since great leaders want to emulate the past, we were given symbolism in architecture to remember. Not only in our buildings but in our symbolic houses, the zodiac.

The Greek philosophers, who followed astronomy and astrology, were not only of intellectual sophistication but also possessed an understanding of our known universe in the cosmos. But it too had a Pantheon of Gods, who changed guard from agriculture to war. It became central to the human experience to protect what is "mine."

But since philosophy ruled Greece and so did astronomy, they created a system based on the influence and transits of planets in one's individual chart. The transits of planets can explain vast amounts of urges and projections that become action. Most of these actions are choices but are limited to consciousness. These choices can lead the individual or collective to feel as the victim, and this is a place of powerlessness.

The third chakra, which is yellow, is the manifestation of ego. Living in the past prevents growth where the mind is fixated on the original event. It needs a solution of peace, but it often uses war to attempt to resolve the trauma.

Earlier I mentioned memorial sites and the colonial obsession that Washington, D.C., has perpetuated the religious ideology of Rome. The United States has emulated a false story of truth that ripples across a few millennia and acts out past regression through theater and campaign. And all this etymology is traced to Greece and Athens.

Wherever oil is extracted, we see the destruction of the indigenous. In 2013 Niger, Africa, the Shell Oil Company created the Trans-Niger oil pipeline. Hence, the increased interest in the African "theater," where war plays out and the earth men in power become living memorials to Macbethian legend. Murder and deception became a method to bury guilt and history.

In 2017 the world became a little more aware of the drama of European colonialism and the Army Special Forces role. ODA 3212 was a part of the 3rd Special Forces group training locals in Tonga Tonga, Niger. This elite fighting group left behind four soldiers and their mourning families as they were ambushed by Islamic extremists.

It is as simple as this. The CIA's mission to retrieve Jaime Woodke, a Christian humanitarian in the region, was more important than the indigenous soldiers and those who trained them.

The four Green Berets that were killed all came from "lower" class families, rendering them expendable for the greater good of humanitarianism and colonialism. They were all enlisted men, just like I was, and this was the biggest "ambush" since 1993 in Mogadishu, Somalia, the very incident that made me decide to join the Army.

Kyle Rittenhouse was acquitted of murder charges on day of the lunar eclipse after his defense claimed self-defense.

My perspective is astrologically karma influenced. In other words, we had a lunar eclipse in Taurus, an earth-based sign. Pluto, the planet of the underworld, was retrograde. We essentially saw a boy playing out the trauma drama of a collective DNA theater.

When I was seventeen, I might have been convinced by the Artificial Intelligence of hate to take up arms and fight those who I felt threatened by. Of course, I would have never done it, because I wouldn't want to kill another person and I was taught the responsibility of such. I just wouldn't have brought a gun to a riot. But these days, everyone is being influenced more than we think.

I watched the video of a young teenager not psychologically developed enough to understand himself, his role in the cosmos and the reality of taking someone's life. I saw a fatherless kid raised by video games with an Eddie Haskell vibration. The character that says, "I'm right because my examples of men say I am, my false understanding of religion and masculinity says I am."

The reality is that, in 2020, it wasn't self-defense. It was Second Amendment defense, patriarch defense, and Kyle was in the right. He was defending with his right to bear arms—a white ideal his elders condoned. He became the poster boy for the dark masculine, and he, no doubt, learned all his combat moves on Call of Duty, the video game. The misnomer is that one must take a side, to take a stand against the other and a gun is the tool for this.

Kyle Rittenhouse was and will be the tool. The effort for old men to hang on to oppressive ideas through this youthful psychopath they've encouraged is quite transparent if you really pay attention.

We were distracted with race by left news outlets and by self-defense issues with the right. Which one is it? A race issue, or a gun issue? I maintain that if everything is going to be about social awareness in society, then why not treat the root cause and not the symptoms like western medicine might with a drug addict or criminal.

The problem is that the creators of A.I., and A.I. itself, are sowing chaos and misinformation in order to cause the implosion of the human population. Drone attacks come from the central Sahara Desert in a newly constructed base to control the terrorist warlords that found niches for wealth doing something they have always done. Tribal warlords with Muslim roots have been part of the Bedouin experience for a long time.

Here is how the CIA works. They find drug markets in foreign countries, i.e. poppies in Afghanistan or cocaine in Nicaragua. Then they funnel gun sales to defend and support the business, weaseling a political foothold in the region. This allows for yellow journalism to spin a humanitarian effort.

It usually comes in the form of a true story about the local population being controlled by a warlord or women and children being abused, raped and often killed. Even better, a couple of dead American soldiers in the street after a secret mission goes wrong, due to bad intelligence. Enter the Green Beret A Team to train the local population to fight this oppression with our infantry tactics.

The Pentagon would be morally right to expose and change the archaic views of the antiquated Muslim religion, especially towards women. But they sell liberation, and the people get colonialism and oppression, instead. They package the American dream brand, but the truth is no one can be part of it without the infrastructure of a "developed nation." No nation can develop when warlords steal aid, which isn't limited to food, water, medical supplies, weapons and vehicles.

The war on terror had the enlisted and officers, as well as the people of America, wondering where were the weapons of mass destruction? Why were we in Afghanistan? Why Iraq? And if there was no direct proof, why kill so many people? How can we support men who've sold us out to corporations?

President Bush Sr. was the director of the CIA in the mid- to late-70s. His colonialism approach to drug dealing corrupted the African American youth with crack in the projects. His lust for the continuation of the poppy trade in the golden crescent of Iran, Afghanistan and Pakistan left a nation fighting an unfinished war of ego and power under the guise of Christian humanitarianism.

America and all nations feel justified by religion. It is easy to package a falsehood to those who still believe that others and their gods are inferior. I learned that it isn't America or Americans we as a human race should be concerned about. It is the sons of men who were taught to have war in their hearts by their own fathers. This is a global problem.

I decided to wade further into the murky waters of definition, history and etymology. Conspiracy is rooted in fear on both sides. One side is usually the people fearing that the government is telling lies that threaten their existence. The other is the government fearing an uprising. *Conspire* means originally to breathe together. In short, a conspiracy is a couple of people or more that breathe together against the government. But who is the real threat?

The money trail of the Eugenic practices of a few rich families can be traced back to the Queen of England. The British financed colonization of North America's headwaters was conceived at Yale University and money flowed back to the Nazi Regime. All this has been testified to by the CIA, FBI and world-renowned historians, as well as Dr. R. Bunch and Dr. A. Sutton.

The American death cult of Skull and Bones was crafted to maximize profits, not only through the guise of overseas humanitarianism, but they secretly installed puppet rulers to expand the wealth of European global domination. Selling drugs produced overseas would catalyze a reason for the youth to die not only on foreign soil but domestically. In short, now the conspiracy of a few scared white men with all the money could reduce the population with civil unrest worldwide.

This torch was passed via the internet to Artificial Intelligence, and aerial surveillance will now do what's best for the algorithm of digital surveillance. We will mine Mars and colonize it, because we have the technology and that's what we do. Civil unrest and revolution will be monitored and dealt with through drones and social shaming. All the while, consensus and censorship reveal apathy in the new world of Artificial Intelligence.

"Think for yourself and question authority."

—Timothy Leary

RESOURCE BOOKS

I n addition to classic works, including the Torah, the Bible, the Book of Mormon, the Rig Veda, the Tibetan Book of the Dead, and the Yoga Sutras of Patanjali, the following books provided informational resources:

Alter, R., 1997. *Genesis*. New York: Norton.

Argüelles, J., 1987. *The Mayan Factor*. Santa Fe, N.M.: Bear.

Burman, E., 2004. *The Inquisition*. Stroud: Sutton.

Campbell, J., 1949. *The Hero With A Thousand Faces*. MJF Books.

Coe, M., 2016. *Reading the Maya Glyphs*. Thames & Hudson.

Deuel, L., 1974. *Conquistadors Without Swords*. New York: Schocken Books.

Donnelly, I., 2016. *ATLANTIS*. [Place of publication not identified]: HANSEBOOKS.

Eknath, E. and Nagler, M., 2007. *The Upanishads*: Nilgiri Press.

Eknath, E.,2007. *The Bhagavad Gita*: Nilgiri Press.

Foerster, B., 2018. *Beyond the Black Sea*: Create Space Publishing.

Gilgamesh. and Sandars, N., 1972. *The Epic of Gilgamesh*. Harmondsworth, Middlesex: Penguin Books.

Gollnick, B., 2008. *Reinventing the Lacandón*. Tucson, Ariz.: University of Arizona Press.

Hunter, M. and Ferguson, T., 1950. *Ancient America and the Book of Mormon*. Oakland, Calif.: Kolob Book Co.

Joseph Campbell and David Kudler Johnson E. Fairchild, 2017. *Myths to Live By*. Joseph Campbell Foundation.

Jung, C., Campbell, J. and Hull, R., 1976. *The Portable Jung*. New York: Viking Press.

Jung, C., Henderson, J., Franz, M., Jaffé, A. and Jacobi, J., n.d. *Man and His Symbols*.

Landay, J., 1978. *Dome of the Rock*. New York: Newsweek.

Mann, W., 2004. *The Knights Templar in the New World*. Rochester: Inner Traditions International, Limited.

Mary Magdalene, Kenyon, T. and Sion, J., 2006. *The Magdalen manuscript*. Boulder, CO: Sounds True, Inc.

Melchizedek, D., 1998. *The ancient secret of the Flower of Life*. Flagstaff, AZ: Light Technology Pub.

Melchizedek, D., 2008. *Serpent of light*. San Francisco, CA: Weiser Books.

Milbrath, S., 2000. *Star Gods of the Maya*: University of Chicago Press.

Narby, J., 1999. *The cosmic serpent*. Putnam Publishing.

Ortiz, E., 2014. *The Akashic records*. Weiser Publishing.

Parks, A., 2013. *Eden*. Vincennes: Pahana Books.

Perera, V. and Bruce, R., 1985. *The Last Lords of Palenque*. Berkeley: University of California Press.

Rosas, F., 2005. *Peruvian Myths and Legends*. Ediciones El Lector.

Roys, R., 1960. *The Maya katun prophecies of the Books of Chilam Balam, series 1*. Washington, D.C.: Carnegie Institute of Washington.

Sharer, R. and Traxler, L., 2006. *The Ancient Maya*. Stanford, Calif.: Stanford University Press.

Sotil Galindo, R., 2008. *Iconografía de la cultura Nasca*. Lima, Perú: UAP, Universidad Alas Peruanas.

Stuart, D. and Stuart, G., 2008. *Palenque: eternal city of the Maya*. Londres: Thames & Hudson.

Tedlock, D., 1996. *Popol Vuh*: Touchstone.

Von Däniken, E., 1971. *Chariots of the Gods*: Bantam Publishing.

Wallis, C. *Tantra Illuminated (2nd Edition*. 2013. Mattamayura Press.

White, D., 2019. *The Yoga Sutra of Patanjali*: Princeton University Press.

Yukteswar, 1974. *The holy science*. Los Angeles: Self-Realization Fellowship.

ABOUT THE AUTHOR

E li Coberly is a world traveler and seeker of truth through adventure. At seventeen, he left his small Pacific Northwest town to fulfill his dream of becoming an Army paratrooper. At twenty, he was honorably discharged and began his search for a new dream.

Eli's writing has taken him worldwide to explore a few of the bigger questions of our human existence, and his prophetic worldview combines military service, counterculture, and the anthropology and archeology of the world's religious symbols. He has studied the migration of the indigenous and ingested their medicine, absorbed their art, and embodied their cosmovision.

A yoga therapist, Eli has been a student of yoga for over a decade. When he isn't writing or practicing yoga, Eli can be found examining Tibetan Buddhist tradition, sitting in ceremony with Maya priests, and traversing caves deep in the Belize jungle. He currently resides in Northern California.